In Sync 2

Ingrid Freebairn
Jonathan Bygrave
Judy Copage

PEARSON
Longman

Contents

Contents

Student Book

Contents

1A He goes to my school.

Grammar Simple present
Vocabulary Family; Countries and nationalities
Function Exchange personal information

Get started

1 Look at the photo. Which people do you think are meeting for the first time? Why?

Presentation

2 🎧 1/02 Listen and read along. Who is from Canada?

Carlos: There's Greg! He **goes** to my school. He's on the basketball team. Hi, Greg! How are you?

Greg: Oh, hi, Carlos. I'm fine, thanks.

Carlos: This is Polly, a friend from the youth club.

Polly: Hello, Greg. Nice to meet you.

Greg: You, too.

Carlos: And this is her cousin, Lin. Lin **is** from Canada.

Greg: Canada? Cool! Are you on vacation in Seattle?

Lin: No, I'm not. My dad **works** for a computer company and we're here for a year.

Greg: **Do** you **like** Seattle?

Lin: Yes, I **love** it. It's a really cool city.

Greg: And **do** you **live** . . .?

Lin: Oh, it's a text message from my mother. I have to go. See you later, guys.

Phrases

🎧 1/03 Listen and repeat.

• See you later, • Nice to meet you. • I have to go.
• How are you? • This is • I'm fine.

💡 Solve it!

3 🎧 1/02 Listen again to the conversation. Write the names on the photo.

Comprehension

4 Write *T* for *true*, *F* for *false*, or *NI* for *no information*.

__T__ 1 Greg and Carlos are at the same school.

_____ 2 Polly is Greg's best friend.

_____ 3 Lin and Polly are cousins.

_____ 4 Lin likes Seattle.

A

B [_____] **C** [_____] **D** [*Greg*_____]

Vocabulary: Family

5 Review. Write as many family words as you can in your notebook. Then check the Word bank on page 124.

6 Complete the sentence.

Lin's father is Polly's _____.

Vocabulary: Countries and nationalities

7a Review. Complete the names of the countries. Then write the nationality adjective for each country. Go to the Word bank on page 124 and check your answers.

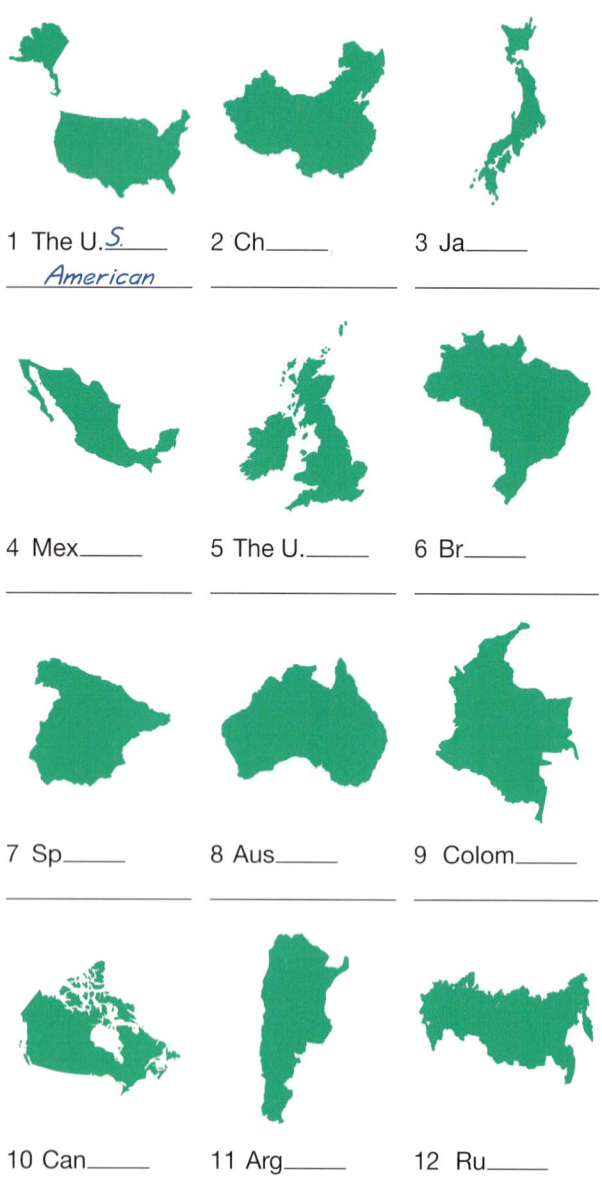

1 The U.*S.* _____
American

2 Ch_____

3 Ja_____

4 Mex_____

5 The U._____

6 Br_____

7 Sp_____

8 Aus_____

9 Colom_____

10 Can_____

11 Arg_____

12 Ru_____

b Extension. List any other countries you know in your notebook.

Presentation

8 [1 04] Listen and read along. What city is Lin from?

Greg: Your cousin's really cool, Polly.

Polly: I know, and she's smart, too. She **speaks** English and Chinese.

Greg: Chinese?

Polly: Yes, her mother **is** from China, but her father's Canadian. He's my dad's brother.

Greg: **Does** he **speak** Chinese, too?

Polly: No, he **doesn't**. He only **speaks** English.

Greg: Where do they **live** in Canada?

Polly: They **live** in Toronto.

Grammar

Simple present	
Affirmative	**Negative**
I **live** in Seattle. He **speaks** English.	I **don't live** in Toronto. He **doesn't speak** Chinese.
Questions	**Short answers**
Do you **live** here? **Does** he **live** here? Where **do** you **live**?	Yes, I **do**./No, I **don't**. Yes, he **does**./No, he **doesn't**. In Seattle.

☛ Go to page 128, Master your grammar.

Basketball Team FACTFILE

	Greg	Marta	Tom
Home city	Seattle, U.S.	Mexico City, Mexico	Quebec, Canada
Languages	English	Spanish and English	English and French
Parents' place of work	father: in a factory mother: in an office	father: in a store mother: in a hospital	father: in a school mother: in a coffee shop

Practice

9a Look at the basketball team factfile. Ask and answer about Greg.

1 What nationality/be/Greg?
   A: *What nationality is Greg?*
   B: *He's American.*

2 Where/be from?
   A: _____
   B: _____

3 What languages/speak?
   A: _____
   B: _____

4 Where/parents/work?
   A: _____
   B: _____

b Now ask about Marta and Tom.

c Make true sentences.

1 Greg and his family/live/in Mexico City.
   Greg and his family don't live in Mexico City. They live in Seattle.

2 Tom/speak/Spanish
_____

3 Tom's father/work/in a store
_____

4 Marta/speak/French
_____

5 Tom and his family/live/in Seattle
_____

Pronunciation: /ɪ/ live, /i/ leave

10 Go to page 126.

Speak

11a Complete the conversation.

Mark: Where are you from?
Lin: *I'm from . . .*
Mark: Is your family <u>Canadian</u>, too?
Lin: _____
Mark: Do you live in <u>Canada</u> now?
Lin: _____
Mark: Do you like <u>Seattle</u>?
Lin: _____
Mark: What languages do you speak?
Lin: _____

b PAIRS Ask and answer questions from Exercise 11a. Change the <u>underlined</u> words.

Write

12 On a piece of paper, write a paragraph about your partner.

Manuel is from Colombia . . .

 Extra practice
- Student Book, page 112, Lesson 1A
- Language Builder: WB, page 2; GB, page 100
- Student CD-ROM, Unit 1

5

I usually go to bed at ten.

Grammar	Adverbs and expressions of frequency
Vocabulary	Daily routines; the time
Function	Talk about daily routines

Get started

1 What is a "daily routine"?

Vocabulary: Daily routines

2 Review. Which phrases do you know for daily routines? Check the Word bank on page 124.

Read

3 🔊 Listen and read along. Who studies more, Lin or Wei? _____

Comprehension

4 Answer the questions with *L* (Lin), *W* (Wei), or *B* (both). Who . . .

__W__ 1 gets up first?

_____ 2 gets home first?

_____ 3 has a long lunch break?

_____ 4 does homework in the evening?

_____ 5 goes to bed first?

_____ 6 studies a lot on weekends?

YOUR WORLD

Lin goes to school in Seattle. Her Chinese cousin, Wei, goes to school in Shanghai.

Lin

"I **always** get up at 7:30 A.M. School starts at 9 A.M. and ends at 3:20 P.M. Lunch is at 12:45. We have an hour for lunch. I **usually** get home from school at about 4 P.M. and I have a snack. Then I do my homework and we have dinner at 6:30. I **often** watch television in the evening, but I go to my cousin Polly's house **once or twice a week**. I **usually** go to bed at about 10 P.M. I **hardly ever** study on weekends. Weekends are for relaxing!"

Wei

"I get up at 6:15 A.M. **every morning**. Classes start at 8 A.M. I'm **hardly ever** late for school. We have a break of two hours at lunchtime. Afternoon classes start at 2 P.M. and end at 6 P.M. I get home and have dinner and then I do two hours of homework. My mother **sometimes** gives me extra homework! I **never** go out during the week. I'm **usually** in bed at 9:30 P.M. I **always** study for about six hours on weekends."

 Solve it!

5 What time does lunch end at Lin's school? What time does lunch start at Wei's school?

Grammar

Adverbs and expressions of frequency

Adverbs of frequency

always usually often sometimes hardly ever never

I **usually** get home at about 4 P.M.

I **hardly ever** go out during the week.

NOTE: I **never get up** late. I **am never** late.

Expressions of frequency

How often do you watch television?

I watch it	**every**	day/morning/afternoon/evening.
	once a	
	twice a	day/week/month/year.
	three times a	

☛ Go to page 128, Master your grammar.

Practice

6 Rearrange the words to make sentences.

1 twice | my | brush | a | I | day. | teeth

I brush my teeth twice a day.

2 hardly | to | sleep | goes | He | ever | 10 P.M. | before

_____

3 you | Do | listen | to | often | in | bed? | music

_____

4 at | school. | does | homework. | her | often | Karen

_____

5 Brazil | to | on vacation | They | go | year. | every

_____

6 never | is | Arturo | for school. | late

_____

Vocabulary: The time

7 **Review.** Say the times in the text about Lin and Wei two different ways. Then check the Word bank on page 124.

7:30 A.M.—seven thirty A.M.; half past seven in the morning

9 A.M.—nine A.M.; nine o'clock

9:15 A.M.—nine fifteen A.M.; a quarter after nine; a quarter past nine

Listen

8 🎧 08 Monica is talking to a fitness instructor. Listen and complete the form.

The Fitness and Fun Gym

New members' fitness form

¹ **Name:** *Monica Evans* ² **Age:** _____

³ **Occupation:** _____

What time does the new member:

⁴ get up? _____

⁵ go to bed? _____

How often does the new member:

⁶ miss breakfast? _____

⁷ have salad for lunch? _____

⁸ have a snack between meals? _____

⁹ What kind of snack? _____

¹⁰ exercise? _____

¹¹ What kind of exercise? _____

Speak

9 **PAIRS** Ask and answer questions from Exercise 8.

A: *What time do you get up?*

B: *I get up at 7:00 from Monday to Friday, but on weekends I get up at 8:30.*

Write

10 On a piece of paper, write about your partner's daily routine.

George usually gets up at about seven o'clock . . .

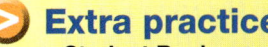

> ### Extra practice
> • Student Book, page 112, Lesson 1B
> • Language Builder: WB, page 4; GB, page 100
> • Student CD-ROM, Unit 1

1c We're having a barbecue.

Grammar Present continuous
Vocabulary Leisure activities
Function Make and respond to requests

Get started

1 Many American teens have their own web pages. What do you think they use them for?

File   Edit   View   Favorites   Tools   Help

MyPlace.co.net   Carlos2020 is logged on

Carlos's photos

This is Greg and me. We**'re playing** basketball.

Polly and Lin **are shopping**, of course! And Polly**'s listening** to music on her cell phone.

This is my little brother Alex. He **isn't doing** his homework. He**'s playing** video games!

Sunday at home. We **aren't having** lunch in the kitchen today. We**'re having** a barbecue outside.

Carlos's messages

Carlos2020 to TomTom:
Hi Tom! What **are** you **doing** right now?

TomTom to Carlos2020:
I**'m not doing** much right now. I**'m chatting** with you!

Carlos2020 to TomTom:
Look at my cool photos! Can you send me a photo of you?

TomTom to Carlos2020:
Sure! No problem. Great photos!

Read

2 Listen and read along. Who is Alex?

Comprehension

3 Answer the questions. Give short answers.

1 What are Greg and Carlos playing? __basketball__
2 Do Polly and Lin often go shopping? _____
3 Where does Carlos usually have lunch? _____
4 What does Carlos want from Tom? _____

Vocabulary: Leisure activities

4a **Review.** In your notebook, list the leisure activities on Carlos's web page and other activities. Then check the Word bank on page 124.

1 *play basketball*

b **PAIRS** Talk about how often you do your favorite activities.

I go skateboarding once or twice a week.

8

 **Solve it!**

5 Look at the photos on page 8. What are Alex's two favorite activities?

Grammar

Present continuous

Affirmative

I**'m playing** basketball right now.
He**'s playing** a video game now.
We**'re having** a barbecue outside today.

Negative

I**'m not watching** TV.
He **isn't doing** his homework.
We **aren't having** lunch in the kitchen.

Questions	Short answers
Are you **playing** basketball?	Yes, I **am**./ No, I**'m not**.
Is he **playing** a game?	Yes, he **is**./ No, he **isn't**.
Are you **having** a barbecue?	Yes, we **are**./ No, we **aren't**.
What are they **doing**?	They**'re eating**.

☞ Go to page 128, Master your grammar.

Practice

6 Write sentences in your notebook.

1 We/not/play football. We/play basketball.
We aren't playing football. We're playing basketball.

2 Alex/not/surf the net. He/play a video game.

3 Polly and Lin/not/sleep. They/shop.

4 Carlos and his family/not/eat in the kitchen. They/have barbecue outside.

7 Now ask questions about the photos on Carlos's web page. Use the cues below.

1 Greg/play football?
A: *Is Greg playing football?* B: *No, he isn't.*
A: *What's he doing?* B: *He's playing basketball.*

2 Alex/watch TV? 3 Polly and Lin/swim? 4 Polly/listen to a CD player? 5 Tom/read a magazine?

Use your English: Make and respond to requests

8 (1 10) **PAIRS** Listen and repeat. Then practice the conversation.

A: Can you take a photo of me, please?
B: Sure. No problem.
A: Thank you! And could you e-mail it to me?
B: I'm sorry, I can't. I'm late for my guitar lesson.
A: OK. Never mind.

Make a request
• Can you take a photo of me, please?
• Could you e-mail it to me, please?

Agree to a request
• Yes, of course./Yes, certainly.
• Sure. No problem.

Respond
• Thank you!/Thanks!

Refuse with a reason
• I'm sorry, I can't. I'm late for my guitar lesson.

Respond
• OK. Never mind.

9 Practice similar conversations. Use the cues. Agree or refuse with a reason.

1 open the window 2 lend me $5 3 buy me a soda

Write

10 On a piece of paper, write your own web page. Use Carlos's web page as a model. Use the present continuous.

> **Extra practice**
> • **Student Book, page 113, Lesson 1C**
> • **Language Builder: WB, page 6; GB, page 101**
> • **Student CD-ROM, Unit 1**

Across cultures

Free-time factfile

American and British teenagers

Sports
In the U.S., football, basketball, and baseball are popular. In the U.K., soccer, rugby, tennis, and basketball are the most popular sports for teenagers.

The Internet and television
Teenagers in both the U.S. and the U.K. today watch television less than before, but they use the Internet more. They spend over 25 hours a week online.

Allowance and shopping
Most American teenagers get an allowance of $15 a week. The average teenager in the U.K. gets about seven pounds (£7) a week. They spend their money on clothes and going out, but magazines, presents, and snacks are also important.

Friends
The average American and British teenager has seven close friends and 16 online friends.

In my free time, I usually play video games or I chat with my friends online. On weekends, I hang out with my friends in town in the local shopping mall.

Danny, 15, Los Angeles, the U.S.

I go swimming twice a week after school, and I go to the movies with my friends once a week, usually on the weekend.

Hannah, 14, Bristol, the U.K.

Get started

1 How important are these things to you? Put them in order: 1 = most important, 5 = least important.

_____ sports   _____ shopping
_____ music   _____ TV
_____ computers   _____ friends and family

New words and phrases
• baseball • less • spend (time) • allowance
• spend money on • close (friend) • local
• shopping mall

Read

2 Read the factfile. Make a list of the teenagers' activities in your notebook.

Comprehension

3 Answer the questions about British and American teenagers.

1 What sports do they play? *soccer, rugby . . .*
2 How long do they spend online?
3 How much allowance do they get?
4 What do they spend it on?
5 How many online friends do they have?

Listen

4 Listen to Nell, Cody, Lauren, and Louis. Write their names under the activities they like.

Cody

Speak

5 **PAIRS** Ask the questions in the Free-time quiz below. In your notebook, write your partner's answers.

A: *Do you play a sport in your free time?*
B: *Yes, I do .*
A: *Which sport do you play? . . .*

FREE-TIME QUIZ

Topics	Questions
Sports	Do you play a sport? (Which?)
Television	Do you watch television? (Which shows?)
The Internet	Do you surf the Internet? (How often?)
Allowance	Do you get an allowance? (How much?)
Shopping	What do you buy with your allowance?
Friends	How many close friends and online friends do you have?

Write

> **Writing tip: Conjunctions *and, or, but, so, because***
>
> We can join two ideas in one sentence by using conjunctions such as *and, or, but, so,* and *because.*
>
> On Monday I go to school **and** my friend's house.
>
> On Saturday we go shopping **or** to the movies.
>
> I sometimes watch TV, **but** I often do other things.
>
> I'm not usually tired, **so** I often go to bed late.
>
> I have a snack after school **because** I'm hungry.

6 Combine the sentences with *and, or, but, so,* or *because.*

1 Is this your DVD? Is it your sister's DVD?
Is this your DVD or is it your sister's DVD?

2 She's always tired. She goes to bed late.

_____

3 In the morning he gets up. He takes a shower.

_____

4 He's in bed. He can't come to the phone.

_____

> **Learning strategy: Review your work**
> Ask yourself:
> • Are my grammar and spelling correct?
> • Did I use conjunctions?

7 On a piece of paper, write your own answers to the Free-time quiz. Try to use *and, or, but, so,* or *because* in your sentences. Then review your work.

I play football twice a week after school, but my favorite sport is basketball.

CLIL PROJECT, page 140

People are watching me.

Grammar	Simple present and present continuous
Vocabulary	Jobs
Function	Talk about jobs

My world

2

Dream job for a day:
TV presenter

This week's contest winner is Tina Valdez from Miami, Florida. Her prize is to do her dream job for a day. This is her diary for that day.

Monday, October 7

6:30 A.M. My dad usually **takes** me to school, but today he**'s taking** me to the Museum of Flight in Seattle, Washington. I'm going to present a science show for teenagers. I **like** science, but I **don't like** early mornings!!!

11:00 A.M. I **wear** T-shirts and jeans during the week, but today I**'m wearing** a yellow shirt and a skirt. The director **doesn't like** my shirt. "Yellow isn't a good color on TV," he says. "Do you have a blue shirt?"

2:00 P.M. I**'m standing** outside the museum. People **are watching** me and I'm very nervous. The director says, "Smile and talk slowly."

5:30 P.M. It's 5:30 now and we**'re** still **working** in the museum. I usually get home at 4:30. But at last I'm starting to enjoy this job!

Get started

1 Look at the photos. What is the girl holding? Why?

Read

2 🎧 12 Listen and read along. Complete the chart.

Photos	1	2	3
Times	*2:00 p.m.*		

Comprehension

3 Answer the questions. Who . . .

1 is taking Tina to the museum? ___*Tina's dad*___
2 doesn't like early mornings? _____
3 doesn't like Tina's shirt? _____
4 tells Tina to smile? _____
5 usually gets home before five? _____

Grammar

Simple present	Present continuous
My dad usually **takes** me to school.	He**'s taking** me to the museum today.
I **wear** jeans every day.	I**'m wearing** a yellow shirt now.

☛ Go to page 129, Master your grammar.

Practice

4 Look at the table below about people doing their "Dream jobs for a day." Make sentences with the simple present or present continuous form of the verbs.

Name	Routine	How often?	Today	Dream Job
Ken	(drive) a taxi	usually	(fly) a plane	
Jenny	(write) e-mails to her friends	every day	(write) a story for a magazine	
Rebecca	(walk) the dog	every Sunday	(help) sick animals	

1 *Ken usually drives a taxi, but today he's flying a plane.*

2 _____

3 _____

Vocabulary: Jobs

5a **Review.** Complete the words to make jobs. Then check the Word bank on page 124.

1 *h* ousewif *e*   2 ___eache___   3 ___octo___   4 ___lumbe___
5 ___dministrative ___ssistant 6 ___cto___   7 ___urs___
8 ___rtis___ 9 ___he___ 10 ___eporte___ 11 ___ode___
12 ___arme___ 13 ___uilde___   14 ___lectricia___
15 ___usicia___ 16 ___olic___ ___ffice___
17 ___aite___/___aitres___ 18 ___tor___ ___ssistan___

b **Extension.** Listen and repeat. Then answer the questions. Who do you go to when . . .

> • beautician • carpenter • cashier • dentist • detective
> • director • engineer • firefighter • hairdresser
> • journalist • mechanic • pilot • politician • receptionist
> • ski instructor • taxi driver • TV presenter • vet

1 you have a problem with your teeth? ____*a dentist*____
2 your cat is sick? _____
3 you have a problem with your car? _____
4 you want a new cupboard? _____
5 your hair is too long? _____
6 you want to go to the station? _____

Solve it!

6 Look at Exercise 4 again. Complete the "Dream Job" part of the chart.

Speak

7 **GROUPS** Game: Mime a job. The other students must ask *Yes/No* questions to find out the job.

A: *Are you serving food now?*
B: *No, I'm not.*
A: *Do you work in an office?*
B: *No, I don't . . .*

Write

8 Imagine you are doing your dream job for a day. On a piece of paper, write a diary entry. Use Tina's diary as a model.

Dream job for a day: A pilot

Saturday, November 5

8 A.M. I usually . . .

> **Extra practice**
> • **Student Book, page 113, Lesson 2A**
> • **Language Builder: WB, page 10; GB, page 103**
> • **Student CD-ROM, Unit 2**

Where are yours?

Grammar	whose . . .?, Possessive 's and s'
	Possessive adjectives and pronouns
Vocabulary	Money; Everyday objects
Function	Shopping at a store

Get started

1 Where are the people in the photo? Why do you think they are there?

Presentation

2 🎧 1/14 Listen and read along. What does Carlos buy?

Carlos and Polly are at the local sports center.

Carlos:	Do you have an extra pair of swimming goggles?
Polly:	No, I don't. Where are **yours**?
Carlos:	They're at school with all my swimming stuff.
Polly:	So **whose** swim shorts are those?
Carlos:	They're my **brother's**, and this is my **parents'** towel.

In the store at the sports center.

Assistant:	Hello. Can I help you?
Carlos:	Yes, please. Do you have any goggles?
Assistant:	Sure. Try these.
Carlos:	How much are they?
Assistant:	They're $10, but there's a 10% discount on swimming stuff today.
Carlos:	Great, I'll take them. And can I have a bottle of water, too, please?
Assistant:	Of course. The water's $1.
Carlos:	Oh, no. My wallet's at school, too. Polly, can I borrow some money?

Comprehension

3 Answer the questions.

1 Where are Carlos's goggles?
   ___*at school*___

2 Who do the swim shorts and towel belong to? _____

3 Why does Carlos want to borrow money? _____

Pronunciation: /ð/ th is, /θ/ think

4 🎧 Go to page 126.

Vocabulary: Money

5 🎧 1/17 Review. Look at Money in the Word bank on page 124 and say these prices. Then listen and check.

1) $5.50 2) 37¢ 3) $8.99 4) 20¢
5) $45 6) $11.75

💡 Solve it!

6 How much does Carlos need to borrow?

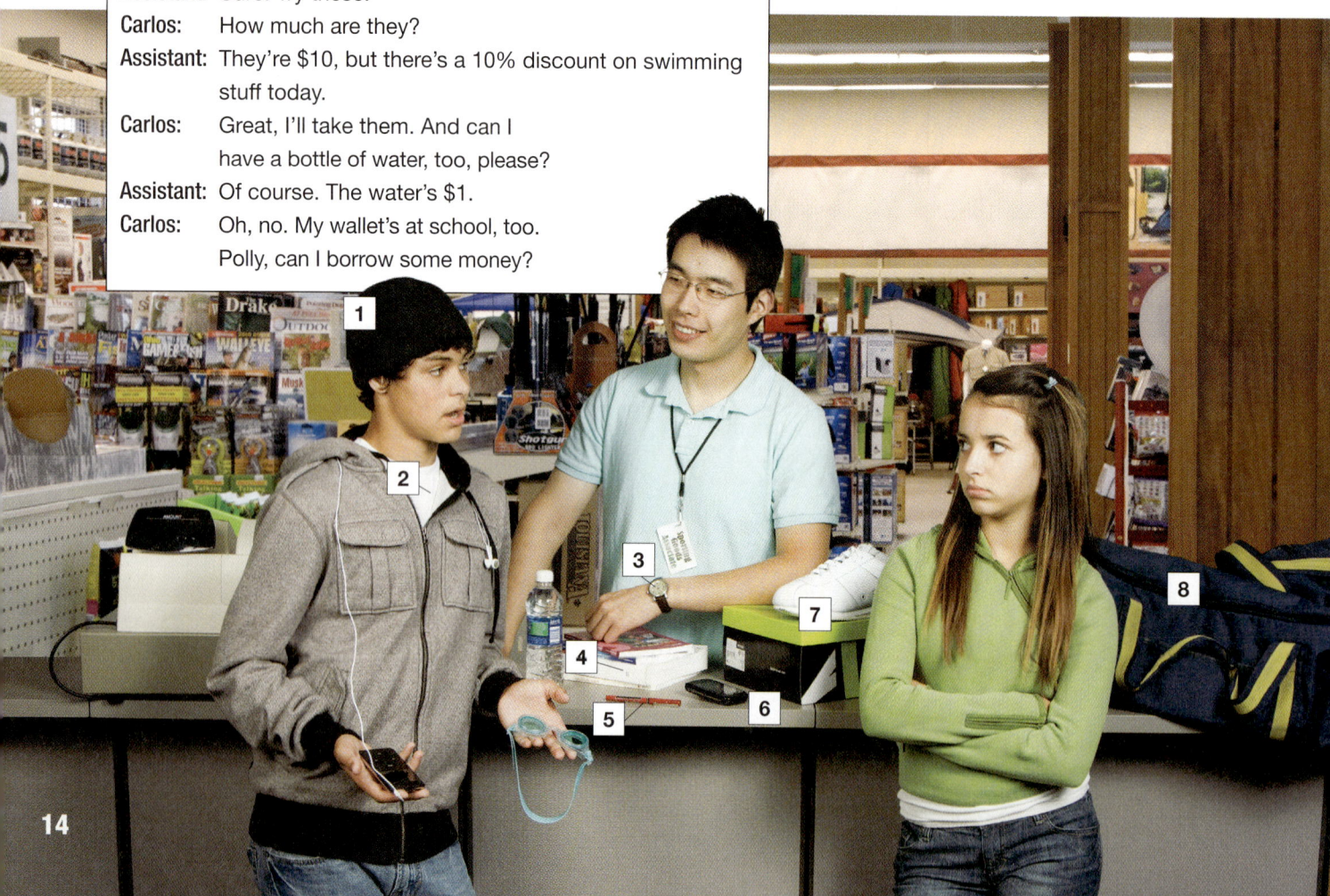

Vocabulary: Everyday objects

7a Review. Look at numbers 1–8 on the photo and name the objects. Then check the Word bank on page 124.

b 🎧 1/18 Extension. Listen and repeat. Underline the items below that are in the photo.

> • battery • belt • bracelet • earring(s)
> • flip-flops • goggles • radio • sunglasses
> • towel • wallet • water bottle

Grammar

whose . . . ?, Possessive *'s* and *s'*	
Whose towel is that?	
Whose swim shorts are those?	

Singular	Plural
It's my brother**'s** bag.	It's my parents**'** towel.
It's my brother**'s**.	It's my parents**'**.

Possessive adjectives		Possessive pronouns	
my	our	mine	ours
your	your	yours	yours
his	their	his	theirs
her		hers	

☛ Go to page 129, Master your grammar.

Practice

8 PAIRS Ask and answer *whose* questions. Use the cues.

A: *Whose camera is this? Is it Julie's?*
B: *No, it isn't hers. It's mine.*

1 Julie/my 2 Harry/my parents 3 your friends/our

4 your mom/Simona 5 Jack/my dad 6 you/his

Use your English: Shop at a store

9 🎧 1/19 PAIRS Listen and repeat. Then practice the conversation

Assistant: Hello. Can I help you?
Carlos: Yes, please. Do you have any goggles?
Assistant: Sure. Try these.
Carlos: How much are they?
Assistant: They're $10.
Carlos: Great, I'll take them. And can I have a bottle of water, too, please?

Offer to help	Ask for something
• Can I help you?	• Do you have any . . .?
	• Can I have a . . .?

Respond	Ask the price
• Yes, sure/certainly/ of course.	• How much is it?
• I'm sorry, we don't have any.	• How much are they?

Respond	Decide
• It's $2.99.	• OK, I'll take it/them.
• They're $5 (each).	• No, thanks.

10 PAIRS Practice similar conversations in other stores. Use the information below.

> 1 a DVD ($11.99) + a blank CD (99¢)
> 2 a digital radio ($57) + four batteries ($3.50)
> 3 a sports bag ($8.85) + sunglasses ($4.99)

Write

11 On a piece of paper, write a shopping list of ten things you need for a vacation. Find out the price of each item.

Shopping list for my vacation
swim shorts $10

> ▶ **Extra practice**
> • **Student Book, page 113, Lesson 2B**
> • **Language Builder: WB, page 12; GB, page 103**
> • **Student CD-ROM, Unit 2**

Grammar	Count and noncount nouns with *some, any,* and *no*
Vocabulary	Food and drink
Function	Talk about food

Get started

1 What is your favorite food?

Vocabulary: Food and drink

2a **Review.** In your notebook, list all the food and drink words you can think of in one minute. Then check the Word bank on page 124.

b 🎧 1/20 **Extension.** Listen and repeat. Then find the foods in the photo below. Match the items in the photo to the food items in the box. Which items are not in the photo?

___ beans	___ beef	___ cake	___ chicken	___ lettuce
___ melon	___ milk	___ mushrooms	___ nuts	
___ olives	___ olive oil	___ peas	___ peaches	
___ pears	___ strawberries	_1_ vinegar	___ yogurt	

C Write the food words in each part of the chart. Can you add any more words?

Fruit	melon,
Vegetables	beans,
Dairy foods	milk,
Meat	beef,
Other	

Presentation

3 🎧 ¹²¹ Listen and read along. What's in the bottle?

Greg: I'm hungry. Are there **any** cookies?

Polly: Um, no, there aren't. There are **no** cookies, and there aren't **any** chips, but there are **some** cheese sandwiches.

Greg: Is there **any** meat?

Polly: Yes, there's **some** chicken. And here are **some** tomatoes.

Greg: Thanks. Mmm! Good chicken! Is there **any** ketchup?

Polly: Yes, there's a bottle in the bag. Here.

Greg: Great. Yuck! This isn't ketchup!

Polly: Oh, sorry. My fault. It's hot chili sauce!

Comprehension

4 Read the conversation again. What food do Polly and Greg have? Put a checkmark (✓) or ✗ next to the words.

1 cookies ✗ 2 tomatoes 3 sandwiches 4 chips
5 chicken

Grammar

Count and noncount nouns with *some, any,* and *no*

Count – plural	Noncount
Affirmative	
There are **some** sandwiches.	There's **some** chicken.
Negative	
There aren't **any** cookies.	There isn't **any** beef.
There are **no** cookies.	There's **no** beef.
Questions	
Are there **any** chips?	Is there **any** meat?

Note: Noncount nouns have no plural form.

☛ Go to page 129, Master your grammar.

Practice

5 Look at the words in Exercise 2b. Underline the count nouns and circle the noncount nouns.

beans (beef)

Speak

6a **PAIRS** Use the words to ask and answer.

1 **A:** *Are there any peaches?* 2 **A:** *Is there any salt?*
   B: *Yes, there are.*   **B:** *No, there isn't.*

1 peaches (✓)	4 cookies (✗)	7 tomatoes (✗)
2 salt (✗)	5 sugar (✓)	8 butter (✗)
3 yogurt (✓)	6 vinegar (✗)	9 beans (✓)

b Say what there is and isn't.

There are some peaches.   *There isn't any salt.*

Listen

7 🎧 ¹²² Listen to Carlos and his mother. Write a shopping list for Carlos in your notebook.

Write

8 On a piece of paper, make a list of items for a picnic. Write about your picnic.

There's a . . . There's some . . . There are some . . .

> **Extra practice**
> • **Student Book, page 114, Lesson 2C**
> • **Language Builder: WB, page 14; GB, page 104**
> • **Student CD-ROM, Unit 2**

INTEGRATED CONSOLIDATION SKILLS

Curriculum link: Geography

Before you read, go to page 19.

Where our food comes from

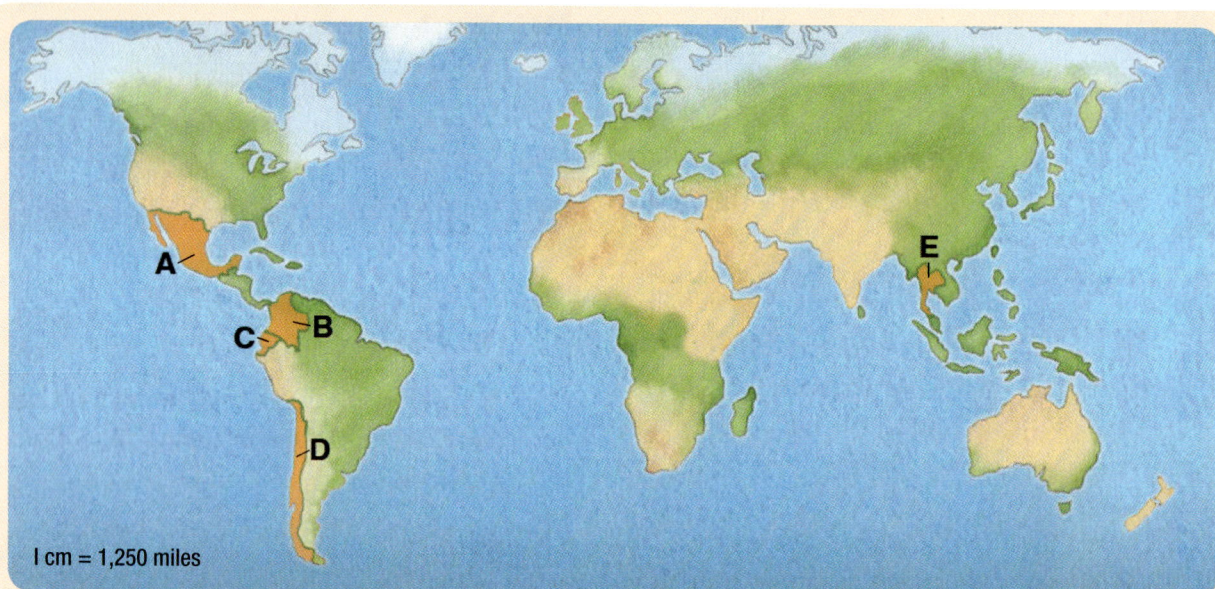

I cm = 1,250 miles

In the U.S. today, there are many different kinds of food in the supermarket. People buy tomatoes, oranges, and strawberries at any time of the year. In many parts of the U.S., this kind of food only grows in the summer, so in autumn, winter, and spring, it often comes from other countries.

Let's look at a typical example. In the photos on page 19, the coffee comes from Colombia, the shrimp comes from Thailand, the tomatoes come from Mexico, the grapes from Chile, and the bananas from Ecuador. All this food travels thousands of miles to your dinner plate. Trucks, ships, and planes use a lot of fuel to carry food around the world. That's a problem for the planet.

Here's what some of our readers say:

My dad's growing potatoes, beans, and tomatoes in our backyard this year. If you can, it's a good idea to grow your own vegetables.
—**Steve, from Ann Arbor, Michigan**

Mom goes shopping at our local farmers' market every week. The food comes from around here, and it's really cheap!
—**Ceci, from San Antonio, Texas**

We live in an apartment in New York City. We don't have a yard, so our food probably comes from different countries. Sometimes it isn't possible to think about the planet!
—**Sierra, from New York, New York**

New words and phrases
• grow • travel • thousands • plate
• ships • fuel • carry • planet

1 _Colombia_   4 _____
2 _____   5 _____
3 _____

Get started

1 Look at the map on page 18. Can you name the countries? Check your answers at the bottom of the page.

A Mexico

> **Learning strategy: Predict from photos, titles, and maps**
>
> Before you read, look at any photos, titles, and maps. Think about the topic and try to predict what the text is about. This will help you to understand it.

2 Look again at the map, the photos, and the title of the article. What do you think the article is about?

Read

3 Read the article. Match the food (1–5) in the photos to the countries. Write the countries.

Comprehension

4 Read the article again. Complete the sentences.

1 In the U.S., you can buy tomatoes _at any time of year_.
2 Food in the U.S. often comes from _____.
3 _____ thinks that farmers' markets are cheap.
4 _____ lives in New York City.
5 _____ has a backyard.

Listen

5 🔊 1/23 Listen to a conversation in a supermarket. Choose the correct answers.

1 What is the customer buying?
   a) fruit   b) vegetables   c) meat
2 Where are the bananas from?
   a) Ecuador   b) the U.S.   c) Chile
3 Where are the grapes from?
   a) China   b) the U.S.   c) Chile
4 How often does the customer think about where food is from?
   a) never   b) always   c) sometimes

Speak

6a PAIRS Read again what Steve, Ceci, and Sierra say in the article. Which opinions do you agree or disagree with?

I agree with Ceci. It's important to buy food from your local area.

b PAIRS Ask and answer.
• What food do you eat from your country?
• What food do you eat from other countries?

Write

7 Think about some of the fresh food you eat regularly. Look at the map. On a piece of paper, write a paragraph about where your food comes from.

I often eat apples. They come from the U.S. . . .

Review: Units 1 & 2

Grammar (40 points)

1 Complete the sentences with the correct form of the verb in parentheses. Put the adverb of frequency in the correct place. (7 points)

0 Pierre __ (speak) French at school. NEVER

Pierre never speaks French at school.

1 Doctors __ (work) in the evenings. OFTEN

_____

2 We __ (be) at home on Saturdays. ALWAYS

_____

3 What time __ you __ (have) lunch? USUALLY

_____

4 My parents __ (go) to the movies. ONCE A YEAR

_____

_____

5 I __ (be) in bed before 10 P.M. HARDLY EVER

_____

_____

6 __ Ann __ (play) your video games? SOMETIMES

_____

_____

7 Michelle __ (not listen) to the radio. EVERY DAY

_____

_____

2 Use the cues to write questions and answers in the present continuous. (8 points)

0 (Carla/read?) (No/swim)

A: *Is Carla reading?*

B: *No, she isn't. She's swimming.*

1 (Elisa/watch a DVD?) (No/listen to music)

_____

_____

2 (Milly/have a barbecue?) (No/play guitar)

_____

_____

3 (Emma and Adam/skateboard?) (No/play soccer)

_____

_____

4 (Paul and Carl/play a video game?) (No/run)

_____

_____

3 Choose the correct word. (8 points)

Betsy: Megan, is this phone ⁰ a) you?
b) your? c) yours?

Megan: No, it isn't ¹ a) mine. b) my. c) me.

Betsy: Well, ² a) who b) whose c) who's is it?

Megan: Maybe it's ³ a) Tom. b) Tom's. c) Toms'.

Betsy: No, it's pink, and ⁴ a) boy b) boy's
c) boys' phones aren't usually pink.

Megan: Is it ⁵ a) Kelly? b) Kelly's? c) Kellys'?

Betsy: No, it's not ⁶ a) hers. b) her. c) she.

Megan: Maybe it's ⁷ a) our teacher.
b) ours teacher. c) our teacher's.

Ms. Lane: Yes, it's ⁸ a) my. b) mine. c) me. Thanks!

4 Complete the sentences with *there is/are* and *a, an, some, any,* or *no*. (8 points)

0 (coffee ✗) There _____ *isn't any coffee* _____.

00 (eggs ?) Are _____ *there any eggs* _____?

1 (rice ✓) There _____.

2 (lettuce ✗) There _____.

3 (bananas ?) Are _____?

4 (nuts ✓) There _____.

5 (strawberries ✗) There _____.

6 (cheese ?) Is _____?

7 (milk ✗) There _____.

8 (cookies ✗) Sorry, there _____ left.

5 Complete the e-mail. Use the simple present or present continuous. (9 points)

File Edit View Favorites Tools Help

From: Claudia88@hypermail.com
To: Jennyjones@outmail.net
Subject: I'm on vacation!

Hi Jenny,
I'm on vacation with my parents. We⁰ _____ *'re staying* _____ (stay) at a hotel in Puerto Rico. Everybody
¹ _____ (speak) English here, so
I ² _____ (not learn) any Spanish right now!
We usually ³ _____ (go) out every day.
I ⁴ _____ (write) this in a coffee shop. My friend Gabriela ⁵ _____ (work) here every Saturday. She ⁶ _____ (make) sandwiches.
I ⁷ _____ (use) her computer because mine is at home. What ⁸ _____ (you do) right now? ⁹ _____ (you enjoy) your vacation?
E-mail me soon!

Love, Claudia

Vocabulary (40 points)

6 Put the words into the correct group. (19 points)

- French • grandfather • journalist • American • cake
- receptionist • honey • Russian • uncle • yogurt
- politician • British • daughter • engineer • nephew
- Chilean • wife • bread • firefighter • sandwich

Family members	Nationalities	Jobs	Food
	French,		

7 Solve the clues and write the jobs.
Find the hidden job. (7 points)

0 D E N T I S T
1 M H
2 P O
3 S R
4 X V
5 H S
6 T
7 C T

8 Complete the words with syllables from the box.
(7 points)

- el • gles • io • lace • let • ring • tery • top

0 bat *tery*   1 brace____   2 ear____   3 lap____
4 neck____   5 rad____   6 tow____   7 gog____

9 Rearrange the letters to make food words. (7 points)

Fruit	Meat/Fish	Vegetables
0 achep *peach*	3 phirsm ____	5 ape ____
1 arpe ____	4 febe ____	6 aben ____
2 nemol ____		7 uletect ____

Use your English (20 points)

10 Complete each mini-conversation with a phrase from the box. (10 points)

- Never mind. • Sure, no problem.
- Can I help you? • How are you?
- See you later. • How much are they?

0 **A:** Hi, Rachel. How are you?
  B: I'm fine, thanks. ___How are you?___
1 **A:** I like these shoes.
  B: _____
2 **A:** Can you close the door, please?
  B: _____
3 **A:** See you.
  B: Yes, OK. _____
4 **A:** I'm sorry, I can't help you. I'm late for school.
  B: OK. _____
5 **A:** _____
  B: Yes, have you got any batteries?

11 Correct the mistake in each item. (10 points)

0 **A:** Could you help me?
      certainly
  B: Yes, ~~certain~~.

1 **A:** Joe, she is Anna.

  B: Hi, Anna.

2 **A:** I'm sorry I can't come.

  B: It doesn't mind.

3 **A:** Say hello to Marcus.

  B: Hi, Marcus. Nice meet you.

4 **A:** Excuse me, you could open the door for me?

  B: Yes, sure.

5 **A:** The T-shirt is $10.

  B: OK. I take it.

SELF-CHECK	
Grammar	____ /40
Vocabulary	____ /40
Use your English	____ /20
Total score	____ /100

21

3A   I hate losing.

Sports

3

Grammar	Verbs of emotion + gerund form (*-ing*)
Vocabulary	Sports and places
Function	Talk about sports

Get started

1 Do you like sports? How athletic do you think you are?

Read

2 Take the quiz. Circle a), b), or c). Then check your score.

How athletic are you?

1 How often do you exercise?
a) Every day
b) Once or twice a week
c) Never

2 Do you like playing team sports?
a) Yes, I do.
b) I prefer playing individual sports.
c) No, I hate them.

3 Do you mind falling down and getting dirty?
a) No, I don't.
b) Yes, a little.
c) Yes, I hate it.

4 When it's cold and wet, which of these do you prefer doing?
a) Doing some sport outside in the rain
b) Watching sports on TV
c) Listening to music

5 You are playing a team sport at school. How do you feel?
a) I really want to win because I hate losing.
b) I want to win, but I don't mind losing.
c) I want to stop.

SCORE

Mostly a)s: You're crazy about sports, especially team sports. You love winning.

Mostly b)s: You like playing sports, but you have other interests, too.

Mostly c)s: You are not an athletic person. That's all right, but make sure you get some exercise.

1 *rugby field*

2

3

4

5

6

7

22

Vocabulary: Sports and places

3a Review. List sports for each verb below. Then check the Word bank on page 124.

play (ball sports) *basketball,*
go (sports ending in *-ing*) *cycling,*
do (other activities) *athletics,*

b Extension. Listen and repeat. Label each picture on page 22 with a sport and a place from the box.

Sports	• basketball • boxing • football • golf • ice skating • go-carting • rugby • soccer • swimming
Places	• course • court • field • pool • ring • rink • track

c Now listen and check your answers to Exercise 3b.

Grammar

Verbs of emotion + gerund (*-ing* form)

They **love watching** sports on TV.
Do you **like playing** team sports?
I **enjoy playing** sports outside.
I **don't mind getting** dirty.
She **doesn't like watching** football.
She **hates falling down**.
He **prefers listening to** music.

☛ Go to page 130, Master your grammar.

Practice

4 Complete with verbs + gerunds.

Polly: I ¹*don't like watching* (not/like watch) soccer. I ² _____ (hate/stand) around and ³ _____ (get) cold.

Carlos: Me, too. I ⁴ _____ (prefer/be) indoors. I ⁵ _____ (not mind/ play) soccer—on my computer!

Lin: I think this is fun! Your brother's really good at soccer, Greg. ⁶ _____ (he/like/play) at the back?

Greg: Ha ha! No, he ⁷ _____ (prefer/play) center forward. He ⁸ _____ (like/score) goals!

Lin: Great pass, Toby!

Carlos: Lin, do you really like soccer?

Polly: No, but she ⁹ _____ (not mind/watch) Toby!

Phrases

Listen and repeat.

• Me, too. • Ha ha! • Great pass!
• (He's really) good at (soccer).

5 Listen. You will hear some expressions. Match them with the phrases below that have the same meaning.

Me, too!	Ha ha!	Great pass!	He's really good at . . .
	1		

Speak

6 PAIRS Ask and answer the questions.

1 Do you prefer watching sports or playing them?
2 Which sports do you like watching/playing?
3 If you don't like sports, what do you prefer doing?

Write

7 On a piece of paper, write your entry for a pen pal website.

I like . . . and. . . . I'm good at. . . . My favorite team is . . . on weekends, but I prefer . . . ➤

> **Extra practice**
> • Student Book, page 114, Lesson 3A
> • Language Builder: WB, page 18; GB, page 106
> • Student CD-ROM, Unit 3

Grammar	Imperatives, *must/must not* for rules
Vocabulary	Parts of the body
Function	Talk about rules

Get started

1 How many parts of the body can you name?

Vocabulary: Parts of the body

2 🎧 1/28 Listen and repeat. Then match the numbers in the photos to the words. Which words do not have a number?

___ ankle ___ arm ___ back ___ chest ___ ear ___ elbow ___ eye _1_ face ___ finger ___ foot ___ hair ___ hand ___ head ___ knee ___ leg ___ mouth _2_ neck ___ nose ___ shoulder ___ teeth ___ thumb ___ toe ___ waist ___ wrist

Read

3 🎧 1/29 Listen and read along. Which belt is the more advanced? Orange or brown?

Comprehension

4 Correct the sentences.

1 Beginners wear a ~~green~~ *white* belt.

2 A "dojo" is a karate teacher.

3 For Step 1, stand on your toes.

4 For Step 3, lift the person's arm in front of him or her.

Karate

What is karate?

Karate is a Japanese martial art. Beginners wear a white belt. Then comes yellow, orange, green, brown, and black for very advanced karate students.

Karate is good for self-defense, and it's great exercise, but you must practice with a karate teacher in a "dojo" (a room for practicing karate, judo, etc.).

Step 1

Relax and **bend** your knees. You must stand with both feet on the floor. **Don't stand** on your toes and **don't bend** your back.

Step 2

Now **hold** the other person's wrist with your left hand. **Push** his or her right elbow up with your right hand. **Step back** with your left foot.

Pronunciation: /ɛ/ l<u>e</u>g, /æ/ b<u>a</u>ck

5 🎧 Go to page 126.

💡 **Solve it!**

6 The boy with the green belt is doing one thing wrong in Step 2. What is he doing wrong?

Grammar

Imperatives	
Affirmative	**Negative**
Bend your knees.	**Don't bend** your back.

☛ Go to page 130, Master your grammar.

How to escape if someone holds you around the neck

Someone is standing behind you. He or she is holding your neck with his or her right arm. What must you do? Look at Steps 1–3 below.

Step 3

Stand up and **lift** the person's arm behind his or her back with your left hand. **Put** your right hand on his or her right shoulder. Now you are in control. **Don't push** his or her arm too hard—you must not hurt him or her.

Practice

7 Complete the instructions with imperatives.

1 D<u>on't</u> s<u>it</u> down. S<u>tand</u> up.
2 B_____ your knees. D_____ s_____ on your toes.
3 H_____ his wrist and l_____ your arm.
4 S_____ back with your left foot.
5 D_____ b_____ your back.
6 P_____ your hand on her shoulder.
7 D_____ p_____ her arm too hard.

Listen

8 🔊 1/32 Listen to a gymnastics teacher. Match the exercises to the pictures below.

A = _____   B = _____   C = _1_

Grammar

must/*must not* for rules	
Affirmative	**Negative**
You **must** practice.	You **must not** hurt him.

☛ Go to page 130, Master your grammar.

Practice

9 Complete the rules for the dojo.

1 ___*You must not*___ be late for your class.
2 _____ listen to the teacher's instructions.
3 _____ take drinks or snacks into the dojo.
4 _____ practice without a teacher.
5 _____ wear shoes in the dojo.
6 _____ wash your karate suit every week.

Speak

10 GROUPS Talk about the rules in your school.
We must be at school at 8:30 a.m....

Write

11 On a piece of paper, write a list of the rules you talked about in Exercise 10.

> 🟠 **Extra practice**
> • Student Book, page 114, Lesson 3B
> • Language Builder: WB, page 20; GB, page 106
> • Student CD-ROM, Unit 3

I'm not going to do that again!

Grammar	*be going to* for future plans, intentions, and predictions
Function	Ask for, make, and respond to suggestions

Get started

1 Do you like rides at theme parks? Why or why not?

Presentation

2 🎧 Listen and read along. Why doesn't Lin like the ride?

Polly: What do you want to do next?

Greg: How about going on that ride?

Carlos: Good idea!

Lin: No, thanks. It's too scary. **I'm going to buy** a drink.

Greg: Oh, come on, Lin. You **aren't going to fall out** of it!

Lin: Oh, all right.

* * *

Greg: OK? Hold on tight!

Lin: Ooh! I think **I'm going to be** sick!

* * *

Lin: **I'm not going to do** that again!

Carlos: Greg and I **are going to get** a burger. We're starving.

Polly: Do you want to go on the Tornado later?

Carlos: Yes, that's a great idea!

Polly: Cool! Lin, what about you?

Lin: You're kidding! **I'm going to sit** on that bench. Have fun!

Comprehension

3 Complete the sentences with the correct name(s).

1 _____*Lin*_____ wants to buy a drink.

2 _____ and _____ are hungry.

3 _____ and _____ want to go on the Tornado.

4 _____ doesn't want to go on another ride.

Grammar

be going to for future plans, intentions, and predictions

Affirmative	Negative	Future time phrases
I'm going to go on the ride. She**'s going to sit** on a bench. We**'re going to get** a burger.	**I'm not going to do** that again. She **isn't going to go** on the Tornado. We **aren't going to buy** a drink.	• this morning/afternoon/evening • tonight • tomorrow • tomorrow morning/afternoon/ evening • on Saturday morning • next week/month/year
Questions	**Short answers**	
What **are** you **going to do**? **Are** you **going to come,** too?	Go on the Tornado. Yes, I **am.**/No, I**'m not.**	

☛ Go to page 130, Master your grammar.

Practice

4 What's going to happen? Write sentences using the words in parentheses.

1 I think that egg was bad. (I/be sick)
I'm going to be sick.

2 There are a lot of clouds. (It/rain)
_____

3 Ben never studies. (He/not pass the test)
_____

4 Luz eats chips every day. (She/get heavy)
_____

5 It's cold at the beach. (They/not swim)
_____

5 You're going to have a party on Saturday. Write conversations using the cues.

1 **A:** What/wear? **B:** my new T-shirt
  A: *What are you going to wear?*
  B: *I'm going to wear my new T-shirt.*

2 **A:** Who/invite? **B:** friends from school
  A: _____
  B: _____

3 **A:** you/dance? **B:** No, we ___ . We/play/CDs
  A: _____
  B: _____

4 **A:** What kind of music/play? **B:** rock music
  A: _____
  B: _____

Use your English: Ask for, make, and respond to suggestions

6 (1 34) **PAIRS** Listen and repeat. Then practice the conversation.

A: What do you want to do tonight?
B: How about going to the movies?
A: I don't know. I don't feel like it.
B: Well, why don't we watch a DVD?
A: Good idea!

Ask for suggestions
• What do you want to do tonight?

Make suggestions
• Why don't we go . . . ? • Do you want to go . . . ?
• What about going . . . ? • How about watching . . . ?

Respond to suggestions
• Good idea!   • That's a great idea.
• I don't know. (It's kind of boring./I don't feel like it.)
• No, thanks.   • You're kidding!

7 **PAIRS** Practice conversations. Use the cues.

• get a pizza • go for a walk • listen to music

Write

8 On a piece of paper, write a paragraph about what you are going to do this weekend.

I'm going to visit my aunt . . .

Extra practice
• **Student Book, page 115, Lesson 3C**
• **Language Builder: WB, page 22; GB, page 107**
• **Student CD-ROM, Unit 3**

Before you read, go to page 29.

Values for living

Birthday plans

My name's Shawn. I'm holding the basketball in the photo. I play basketball for my school. My coach, Mr. Watts, says that I'm good at basketball.

Mr. Watts: OK, everyone, this is an important game. Good luck!
Diego: We're going to win, and I'm going to score 20 baskets!

Diego is my best friend.

Brett: Hey, Shawn! Don't give the ball to Diego. He stinks!

Brett is a year older than me, and I don't like him. He's sitting with Emma. They're always together. I like her, but she doesn't even know my name.

Shawn: Don't listen to Brett.
Diego: I never listen to Brett. By the way, don't forget about Saturday, Shawn.
Shawn: Of course. It's your birthday. What do you want to do?
Diego: How about going to the movies in the afternoon and then having a pizza?
Shawn: Good idea.

Sixty minutes later the game is over.

Mr. Watts: Good job, Shawn. Twelve baskets!
Diego: Only two baskets for me. That's OK. Don't forget about Saturday, Shawn!
Shawn: Of course not!

Diego leaves, and then I see Emma. She's looking at me and smiling.

Emma: Hi, Shawn. Great job! You're really good at basketball.
Shawn: Thanks. I really love playing it.
Emma: Can you play beach volleyball, too?
Shawn: A little. Why?
Emma: Some friends and I are going to the beach on Saturday, and then we're going to have a barbecue in the evening. Why don't you come?
Shawn: Who's going to be there?
Emma: Me, Brett, Brett's girlfriend, and some other people.
Shawn: Sure. That's a great idea.
Emma: OK. See you on Saturday.

I feel really happy. Then suddenly I remember: It's Diego's birthday on Saturday!

New words and phrases
• true • cancel (v) • plans • tell the truth
• score (v) • basket • by the way
• smile (v) • stink (v) • suddenly

Get started

1 Read the sentences below and check (✔) the ones you agree with. A true friend . . .

_____ a) listens to your problems.

_____ b) doesn't talk about you when you aren't there.

_____ c) never cancels plans.

_____ d) always tells you the truth.

Read

2 Read the first part of a story on page 28. Match the people in the photo with the correct names.

___ Brett ___ Diego ___ Shawn ___ Emma _2_ Mr. Watts

Comprehension

3 Complete with the correct name.

1 Shawn's best friend is _Diego_____.

2 Shawn doesn't like _____.

3 _____ plays well in the game, but _____ doesn't.

4 It's _____ birthday on Saturday.

5 Shawn makes plans to go to the movies with _____.

6 _____ invites Shawn to a beach barbecue.

Speak your mind!

> **Learning strategy: Don't worry about mistakes**
>
> When you speak, try to relax. Don't worry about making mistakes. Just speak!

4 PAIRS What's the right thing for Shawn to do? Choose the best advice. Tell Shawn and say why.

Go to the movies with Diego.

Go to the barbecue with Emma.

Why don't you take Diego with you to the barbecue?

Stewart, 14 **Teresa, 14** **Cassie, 15**

I think Teresa is right. Go to the barbecue with Emma.
Barbecues are fun.

Listen

> **Listening tip: Predict**
>
> Before you listen, try to predict what is going to happen and what people are going to say. This helps you to understand when you listen.

5a Before you listen to the next part of the story, try to predict what is going to happen.

I think Shawn is going to . . .

b 🎧 ¹/₃₅ Listen. Were your predictions correct? Then answer the questions.

1 What does Shawn suggest? _____

2 Does Diego agree? _____

3 What does Diego never do on Shawn's birthday? _____

4 What does Shawn decide to do on Saturday? _____

Write

6 You're Shawn. On a piece of paper, write an e-mail to Emma.

- Thank her for the invitation.
- Say you're sorry you can't come. Explain that it's your friend's birthday and you have movie tickets.
- Suggest going out on another day.

File Edit View Favorites Tools Help

Hi Emma!

_Thanks for the invitation to _____

_I'm really sorry _____

_How about _____

CLIL PROJECT, page 140

Places

4

Grammar	Comparative and superlative forms of adjectives
Vocabulary	Home and furniture
Function	Talk about homes

Get started

1 What is in your house or apartment?

Vocabulary: Home and furniture

2a Review. How many home and furniture words can you remember? Check the Word bank on page 125.

b 🎧 36 Extension. Listen and repeat. Match the numbers on the photo to these parts of the house. Which words are not in the photo?

> **Parts of the house**
> __ balcony __ basement __ ceiling
> __ chimney __ fence __ gate
> __ roof __ stairs __ steps _1_ yard

Read

3 🎧 37 Listen and read along. What did the Lees do on their vacation? _____

Comprehension

4 What does each person think? Put a checkmark (✓) if he or she likes the object and an ✗ if he or she doesn't like it.

Maureen:	✓	✗
1 the balcony	✓	
2 the living room		
3 the kitchen		
4 the house in Costa Rica		
Marcus:		
5 Costa Rica		
6 the Costa Rica weather		
7 the balcony		

Home Exchange in Costa Rica

A home exchange is a good way to take a vacation. It's **cheaper than** a hotel and **more exciting than** a visit to your relatives. The Lee family is staying in a house in Lake Arenal, Costa Rica.

❝This house is **larger than** our house in Seattle. I like the balcony, and the living room is great. **The most disappointing** thing is the kitchen. It's **the smallest** room in the house. But overall, I really like the house.❞

Maureen, 45

❝This is **the most exciting** place in the world! Costa Rica is **more interesting than** the U.S. And it's hotter. I love it! **The best** thing about this house is the balcony.❞

Marcus, 14

Grammar

Comparative and superlative forms of adjectives

Short adjectives

Base form	Comparative	Superlative
cheap	cheap**er**	cheap**est**
big	big**ger**	big**gest**
happy	happ**ier**	happ**iest**

Long adjectives

Base form	Comparative	Superlative
interesting	**more** interesting	**most** interesting

Irregular adjectives

Base form	Comparative	Superlative
good	**better**	**best**
bad	**worse**	**worst**
far	**farther**	**farthest**

It's **cheaper than** a hotel. (comparative)
This is **the most exciting** place in the world. (superlative)

☛ Go to page 131, Master your grammar.

Practice

5a Look at the chart. Write 5 sentences in your notebook about the three vacation homes. Compare them using these adjectives.

• comfortable • expensive • far • large • modern • small

1 *C is more modern than A, but B is the most modern.*

	Home A	Home B	Home C
Year built	1940	2007	1980
Distance from town	3 m	6 m	0 m
Price per week	$525	$950	$700
Size	900 sq ft	500 sq ft	800 sq ft
Comfort	6/10	7/10	8/10

b Which home do you prefer and why?

Pronunciation: /v/ <u>v</u>ase, /w/ <u>w</u>all

6 🎧 Go to page 126.

Listen

7 🎧 Listen to Arturo and Eva from Costa Rica. They are staying in the Lees' house in Seattle. Take notes on what they say about:

1 the kitchen _____
2 the bedrooms _____
3 the bed _____
4 the yard _____
5 the weather _____

Speak

8 Look at your notes for Exercise 7. Do Arturo and Eva like the Lees' house? Give reasons.

A: *I think they don't like the house. The yard is smaller than their yard in Costa Rica . . .*

Write

9 Write a paragraph about Arturo and Eva and their feelings about the house. Use your notes from Exercises 7 and 8.

> **Extra practice**
> • **Student Book, page 115, Lesson 4A**
> • **Language Builder: WB, page 26; GB, page 109**
> • **Student CD-ROM, Unit 4**

There isn't much room.

Grammar Count and noncount nouns
with *much, many, a lot of, a few, a little*
Vocabulary Noncount nouns
Function Ask permission and respond

Get started

1 Look at the photo. What are the people doing? Why?

Presentation

2  Listen and read along. Which town are Polly, Carlos, and Polly's brother Mick going to?

Polly: Mick, can I put my backpack in the trunk?

Mick: Sure, but there isn't **much** space.

Polly: I can see that!

Carlos: Hi, guys. Sorry I'm late. Is it all right if I put my luggage in the trunk, too?

Polly: Wow! How **many** bags do you have?

Mick: OK. Let's go. We don't have **much** time.

Polly: But it's only two o'clock. Is there usually **much** traffic at this time of day?

Mick: Yes, there's always **a lot of** traffic on Friday afternoon.

Carlos: Can we have some music? I have **a few** rap CDs with me.

Polly: Oh, no, not rap music! Is it a long way to Portland, Mick?

Comprehension

3 Answer the questions.

1 What is Polly taking? __a backpack__
2 What time is it? _____
3 What day of the week is it? _____
4 What kind of music does Carlos like? _____

Vocabulary: Noncount nouns

4a  Listen and repeat. Then write these noncount nouns in the correct place in the chart. Which word is not in the chart?

- food • furniture • homework • ~~luggage~~ • money
- music • space • time • traffic • trash

1 *luggage* a suitcase, _____	2 _____ an empty can, _____	3 _____ a chair, _____
4 _____ an egg, _____	5 _____ an exercise, _____	6 _____ a 10¢ coin, _____
7 _____ a car, _____	8 _____ a minute, _____	9 _____ a CD, _____

b Now add another count noun to each list in the table.

1 luggage: a suitcase, *a backpack*

Grammar

Count and noncount nouns with *much, many, a lot of, a few, a little*

Count nouns Affirmative	Noncount nouns Affirmative
There **are a lot of** cars. There **are a few** cars.	There**'s a lot of** traffic. There**'s a little** traffic.
Negative	**Negative**
There **aren't many** cars.	There **isn't much** traffic.
Questions	**Questions**
Are there many cars? **How many cars** are there?	**Is there much** traffic? **How much traffic** is there?

☛ Go to page 131, Master your grammar.

Practice

5 Complete the sentences with *much, many, a lot of, a few,* or *a little.*

1 We don't have _____*much*_____ homework tonight.
2 Are there _____ students in your class?
3 How _____ luggage do you have?
4 How _____ people are there outside?
5 There isn't _____ traffic at night.
6 There are _____ students in this school —2,000!
7 There's _____ money in my wallet, but not much.
8 There are _____ coins in my purse, but not many.

6 Complete the conversation about a party with *much*, *many*, *a lot of*, *a few,* or *a little.*

Greg: How [1] _____*many*_____ people are coming?
Toby: About 30.
Greg: Thirty! That's [2] _____ people!
Toby: I know. And there isn't [3] _____ space in this room.
Greg: How [4] _____ food do we have?
Toby: We have [5] _____ food. At least ten pizzas. But there are only [6] _____ colas in the fridge. We need to buy more.
Greg: OK. What about music? There aren't [7] _____ good CDs here.
Toby: I have [8] _____ dance CDs upstairs.

Use your English: Ask permission and respond

7 🎧 **PAIRS** Listen and repeat. Then practice the conversation.

A: Can I put my bag here?
B: Sure.
A: And is it OK if I sit here?
B: Actually, someone's sitting there. Sorry.

Ask permission
• Can I/May I put my bag/sit here?
• Is it all right/OK if I put my bag/sit here?

Respond positively
• Sure. • Yes, certainly. • Yes, of course.
• No problem!

Respond negatively
• Sorry, no.
• Actually, there isn't much space. Sorry.

8 **PAIRS** Use the cues to practice similar conversations. Then make your own requests.

• borrow your pen • use your dictionary
• leave class early • open the window

Write

9 On a piece of paper, write about things in your classroom. Use *much, many, a lot of, a few,* or *a little.*

In my classroom, there are a lot of students . . .

> **Extra practice**
> • **Student Book, page 115, Lesson 4B**
> • **Language Builder: WB, page 28; GB, page 109**
> • **Student CD-ROM, Unit 4**

4c How high is it?

Grammar Question word *how* + adjectives
of dimension
Vocabulary Large numbers
Function Talk about dimensions

Phrases

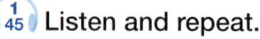 Listen and repeat.

- Give us a break!
- Sorry, I don't have a clue.
- Really? That's interesting.
- It sounds great!

Get started

1 What is *sightseeing*? Where do people sightsee in
your town?

Presentation

2 Listen and read along. What are the friends
doing?

Greg: That's the Space Needle.
Lin: Wow! **How high** is it?
Toby: It's 605 feet high. The observation deck is 520 feet high.
Lin: Really? That's interesting. **How wide** is it?
Toby: It's 120 feet wide.
Greg: It has stores and a revolving restaurant.
Lin: It sounds great! **How many** people visit it every year?
Greg: Sorry, I don't have a clue.
Toby: More than one million. It's the most popular tourist
attraction in the Northwest and . . .
Greg: OK, Toby. Give us a break! This isn't a math class!

Comprehension

3 Correct the mistakes.

1 Greg, Toby, and Lin are ~~shopping~~. *sightseeing*

2 The Space Needle is 520 feet high.

3 People go there to watch soccer.

4 Greg knows the most about the

Space Needle.

34

Vocabulary: Large numbers

4 🔊 ¹⁄₄₆ Listen and repeat the numbers.

190	a hundred and ninety
500	five hundred
675	six hundred and seventy-five
1,000	a thousand
1,280	one thousand two hundred and eighty
10,000	ten thousand
100,000	a hundred thousand
1,000,000	a million
1,000,000,000	a billion

💡 Solve it!

5 Complete the words.

1 There are 12 m _onths_ in a y _____.

2 There are 365 d _____ in a y _____.

3 There are 100 c _____ in a d _____.

4 There are about 8,000,000,000 p _____ in the w _____.

3.28 feet = 1 meter
0.62 mile = 1 kilometer
2.2 pounds = 1 kilo

Grammar

Question word *how* + adjectives of dimension

How high/tall is it?	It's 50 feet **high/tall**.
How long is it?	It's 100 feet **long**.
How wide is it?	It's 356 feet **wide**.
How deep is it?	It's 2 feet **deep**.
How heavy is it? or	
How much does it **weigh**?	**It's/It weighs** 30 pounds.
How far is it?	It's 70 miles.
How big is it?	It's **very big**.

☛ Go to page 131, Master your grammar.

Practice

6 **PAIRS** Look at the chart. Write questions about the dimensions of the places in your notebook.

How high is the Eiffel Tower?

		High	Long	Wide	Deep
	The Eiffel Tower (Paris, France)	1,063 ft (324 m)		about 328 feet (100 m)	
	The Grand Canyon (Arizona, U.S.)		277 miles (446 km)	18 miles (29 km)	5,000 ft (1,524 m)
	The Golden Gate Bridge (San Francisco, U.S.)	750 ft (227 m)	8,981 ft (2,737 m)	89 ft (27 m)	220 ft (67 m)

Speak

7 **PAIRS** Ask and answer the questions in Exercise 6.

A: *How high is the Eiffel Tower?*
B: *It's one thousand and sixty-three feet high.*

Write

8 On a piece of paper, write about the places in Exercise 6 for an online encyclopedia.

1 *The Eiffel Tower is in Paris in France. It's one thousand and sixty-three feet high and . . .*

Extra practice
- Student Book, page 116, Lesson 4C
- Language Builder: WB, page 30; GB, page 110
- Student CD-ROM, Unit 4

35

Before you read, go to page 37.

Across cultures

Famous landmarks of South America

What do you think are the most important modern landmarks in South America? These are our top two choices:

Panama Canal, Panama

I think it's the Panama Canal. It is one of the most important canals in the world. It is 48 miles (77 km) long, and it takes 8–10 hours to sail through it.

Rosa, 14

The Panama Canal joins the Atlantic Ocean with the Pacific Ocean. It is the fastest way for ships to get across South America. The canal is over 100 years old. It cost about $375 million to make. The canal has three sets of locks. Ships pay tolls when they go through the canal. Big ships pay very high tolls, but small ships pay low tolls. Fifteen thousand ships sail through the canal every year!

Itaipu Dam, Brazil and Paraguay

The Itaipu Dam is huge! In fact, it's one of the biggest dams in the world. It's higher than a 64-story building!

Luis, 14

The Itaipu Dam is on the border of Brazil and Paraguay. It is almost 20 years old. It cost $18 billion to build. It is almost 5 miles long. The dam provides 25% of Brazil's electricity. However, it provides most of Paraguay's electricity.

> **New words and phrases**
> • landmark • canal • join • locks • tolls
> • dam • huge • border • provides • electricity

Get started

1 Look at the photos. Do you recognize the places? Where are they?

Read

2 Read the article on page 36. How old is the Panama Canal? The Itaipu Dam? _____

Comprehension

3 Complete the factfile about the landmarks.

	Panama Canal	Itaipu Dam
Where?		
What is it?		
Cost		
Dimensions		

Listen

Learning strategy: Listen more than once

The first time you listen, don't worry about the details. Get the general meaning. Then listen again to note the details.

4 🎧 1/47 Listen to the conversation. Complete Ben's postcard.

Hi!
This is a ¹ _____statue_____ of Christ the Redeemer. It's in Rio de Janeiro, ² _____. It's 130 feet tall, and it looks even taller because it's on top of a big mountain. It's ³ _____ feet wide, and it weighs 635 ⁴ _____! Isn't it beautiful? See you soon!
Ben

Speak

5a Think of a modern landmark in your country. Answer the questions in your notebook.

- What is it?
- Where exactly is it?
- How old is it?
- How tall (wide/deep, etc.) is it?

b GROUPS Describe your landmark. Don't say the name! The group must guess it.

Write

Writing tip: Conjunctions *but* and *however*

We can join two contrasting ideas with *but*. We can also use *however*.

But can join two sentences. It follows a comma.
*Big ships pay high tolls, **but** small ships pay low tolls.*

However usually comes first in a sentence and is followed by a comma.
The dam provides 25% of Brazil's electricity.
However, *it provides most of Paraguay's electricity.*

6 Write sentences with *but* and *however* in your notebook.

1 It takes eight to ten hours to sail through the Panama Canal.
It takes much longer to sail around South America.

It takes eight to ten hours to sail through the Panama Canal, but it takes much longer to sail around South America.

It takes eight to ten hours to sail through the Panama Canal. However, it takes much longer to sail around South America.

2 The Panama Canal has locks. The Itaipu Dam doesn't have locks.

3 The canal is longer than the dam. The dam is taller than the canal.

4 The canal cost $375 million. The dam cost $18 billion.

5 The Itaipu Dam is in Brazil. It is also in Paraguay.

7 On a piece of paper, write about your landmark from Exercise 5. Use the article in Exercise 2 to help you.

The Torre Mayor is the tallest building in Mexico City . . .

CLIL PROJECT, page 140

Grammar (40 points)

1 Rewrite the sentences using the underlined verb and a gerund (*-ing*) form. (12 points)

0 I often watch TV in bed. I <u>love</u> it.
   I love watching TV in bed.

1 I sometimes help Mom to cook. I <u>don't mind</u> it.
   _____

2 I always get up late on Sunday. I <u>love</u> that.
   _____

3 He often plays video games. He <u>enjoys</u> that.
   _____

4 We do our homework together. We <u>like</u> that.
   _____

5 She often lends me money. She <u>doesn't mind</u> that.
   _____

6 I'm sometimes late for school. I <u>don't like</u> that.
   _____

2 Rewrite the sentences with *must* or *must not*. (5 points)

0 NO TALKING! _____ *You must not talk.* _____
1 LEAVE YOUR BAG HERE!
   _____
2 DON'T PLAY MUSIC! _____
3 PUT TRASH IN THE CAN!
   _____
4 NO RUNNING! _____
5 TURN OFF YOUR PHONE!
   _____

3 Complete the sentences with the correct form of *(not) going to*. (6 points)

0 _____ *I'm going to play* _____ (play) a video game.
1 What _____ (you/wear) to Jake's party?
2 It's only six o'clock. We _____ (not/be) late.
3 Surely you _____ (not watch) TV all evening!
4 Emma _____ (not/call) Maria tonight.
5 A: Kevin can't find his passport.
   B: Oh, no! What _____ (he/do)?
6 Bob _____ (not pass) his test.

4 Complete with the comparative or superlative form of the adjectives. (9 points)

0 Canada is _____ *colder than* _____ Mexico. (cold)
00 This is _____ *the oldest* _____ house in the city. (old)
1 English is _____ Russian. (easy)
2 Science is one of _____ subjects. (interesting)
3 Basketball is _____ football. (exciting)
4 Who's _____ actor in the world? (bad)
5 Your T-shirt is _____ my jacket! (expensive)
6 You're _____ father in the world! (good)
7 Which city is _____ from Lima? Miami or Santiago? (far)
8 My new bedroom is _____ my old bedroom. (comfortable)
9 What's _____ room in your house? (big)

5 Circle the correct words. (8 points)

0 I have *much/*(*a lot of*) work to do.
1 We don't have *much/many* time.
2 We don't have *many/much* rock CDs.
3 There's *a lot of/much* trash here.
4 He doesn't have *many/much* money.
5 He has just *a few/a little* coins.
6 Is there *a few/much* traffic in your town?
7 There are *much/a lot of* chairs in this room.
8 How *many/much* people were at the party?

Vocabulary (40 points)

6 Complete with the name of the sport and sports place. (12 points)

You play 0 _____ *soccer* _____ on a
00 f *ield* _____.

You play 1 _____ on a
2 c _____.

You play 3 _____ on a
4 c _____.

You go 5 _____ on a
6 r _____.

You go 7 _____ on a
8 t _____.

You do 9 _____ in a 10 r _____.

You go 11 _____ in a 12 p _____.

7 Circle the word that doesn't belong. (10 points)

0 leg knee foot (head)

1 nose thumb ear mouth

2 ankle hand finger wrist

3 chest waist stomach toe

4 hair toe finger thumb

5 knee elbow neck wrist

8 Complete the words. Match them to the items on the plan. (10 points)

0 B _ALCONY_ 1 R__O__ 2 A__ __IC

3 C__ __M__EY 4 B__ __HR__ __M

5 C__ __L__NG 6 F__N__ __

7 C__ __PUT__ __ 8 ST__ __ __S

9 G__T__ 10 B__SEM__ __T

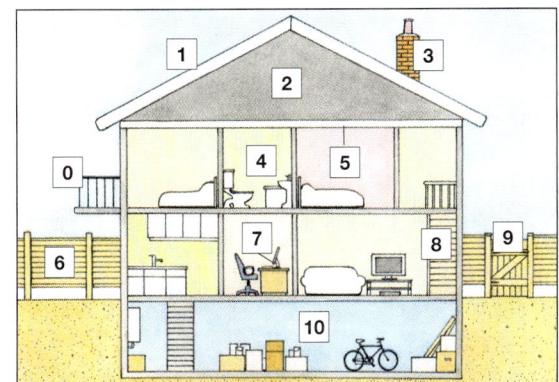

9 Write the correct adjective. (5 points)

0 A: How _____ _tall_ _____ are you?

 B: I'm 5 feet 3 inches.

1 A: How _____ is the building?

 B: It's 500 feet.

2 A: How _____ is the river?

 B: It's 350 miles.

3 A: How _____ is the road?

 B: Only 10 feet.

4 A: How _____ is the pool?

 B: Six feet. You can dive into it.

5 A: How _____ is your suitcase?

 B: It's 40 pounds.

10 Write the numbers. (3 points)

0 250 _two hundred and fifty_

1 1,089 _____

2 74,338 _____

3 32,000,000 _____

Use your English (20 points)

11 Choose the correct response. (10 points)

0 A: I like go-carting.

 B: a) I like it. b)(Me, too.)c) It's for me, too.

1 A: Does Carlos know this video game?

 B: Yes, he's a) good at b) good in c) good for it.

2 A: I'm going to be a famous star.

 B: a) Great pass! b) Ha ha! c) Sorry, I can't.

3 A: It's cold. I don't want to play football.

 B: But it's sunny! a) Don't be silly! b) Great pass!

 c) It sounds great.

4 A: I'm going to sing a song.

 B: No! a) Give us a break! b) Me, too.

 c) Cool.

5 A: What's the name of that movie star?

 B: a) Really? b) Sorry, I don't have a clue. c) OK.

12 Look at the scrambled conversations. Number the lines in the correct order. (10 points)

Conversation 1

_____ a) Thanks. And can you watch my bags for an hour?

_____ b) Yes, of course. No problem. It's over there.

_____ c) Yes, certainly. Put them here near my desk.

_____ d) Sorry. I'm not going to be here.

_1_ e) Can I use your telephone?

_____ f) Oh. Well, can I leave them here for five minutes?

Conversation 2

_____ a) Yes, that's a great idea. Let's go!

_____ b) No, thanks. I don't really feel like swimming today.

_____ c) After lunch? I'm not sure. What do you suggest?

_____ d) OK, not swimming, then. What about go-carting?

_____ e) Do you want to go swimming?

_1_ f) What do you want to do after lunch?

SELF-CHECK	
Grammar	_____ /40
Vocabulary	_____ /40
Use your English	_____ /20
Total score	_____ /100

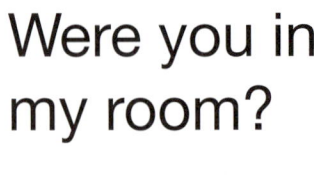

Truth and lies

5A Were you in my room?

Grammar	Simple past of the verb *be* Past adverbial phrases
Vocabulary	Dates
Function	Talk about where you were in the past

Get started

1 Look at the photo. Who is asking, "Were you in my room?"

Presentation

2 🎧 2/02 Listen and read along. Who was in Mexico?

Lin: Toby! You're back! How **was** Mexico?

Toby: It **was** great. I **was** in Mexico City on June 16, Veracruz on June 21, and I was in Monterrey yesterday.

Lin: Cool! I want to go to Mexico.

Toby: Greg, **were** you in my room last week?

Greg: No. Of course not! Why?

Toby: Because my video games are on my bed. Look! They **weren't** there before. They **were** on my chair. Why are they on my bed?

Greg: Dunno. It **wasn't** me!

Toby: And my tennis racket isn't here.

Greg: I don't play tennis.

Toby: Greg, I **wasn't** born yesterday! I'm going out now, and when I get back I want my tennis racket back!

Lin: He's so cool!

Greg: Cool? You're crazy!

Phrases

🎧 2/03 **Listen and repeat.**

- You're crazy! • You're back!
- Of course not! • Dunno.

Comprehension

3 Complete the sentences.

1 Toby plays ____*soccer*____ and _____ .

2 Toby's video games are _____ .

3 Toby can't find _____ .

4 Lin thinks Toby is _____ .

5 Greg thinks Lin is _____ .

 **Solve it!**

4 Look at the photo on page 40. Is Greg telling the truth? How do you know?

Vocabulary: Dates

5 Review. Check the Word bank on page 125. Then say these dates, using ordinal numbers.

- 03/18/1996 • 02/02/2002
- 07/31/2012 • 08/23/1905

Listen

6 🎧 2 04 Listen and write the celebrity birthdays.

1 Robert Pattinson ___*May 13*___

2 Kristen Stewart _____

3 Miley Cyrus _____

4 Ashley Tisdale _____

Grammar

Simple past of the verb *be*

Affirmative	Negative
He **was** in Veracruz.	He **wasn't** in Cancún.
They **were** in Mexico.	They **weren't** in the U.S.
Questions	**Short answers**
Was he in Mexico?	Yes, he **was**./ No, he **wasn't**.
Were they in the U.S.?	Yes, they **were**./ No, they **weren't**.

Past adverbial phrases

- yesterday
- yesterday morning/afternoon/evening
- last night/week/month/year
- last Monday/July

☛ Go to page 132, Master your grammar.

Practice

7a Look at Toby's room <u>before</u> his trip. Then look at the photo on page 40 of his room <u>after</u> his trip. Write five differences in your notebook.

1 Before his trip, Toby's video games were on his chair. After his trip, they weren't on his chair. They were on his bed.

Before Toby's trip

b PAIRS Ask and answer questions about Toby's room before his trip.

A: *Where were his video games before his trip?*
B: *They were on his chair.*

Speak

8 PAIRS Ask and answer questions about where you were and who you were with at these times.

- 9 o'clock yesterday evening
- January 1   • last Sunday

A: *Where were you at nine o'clock?*
B: *I was at home with my family.*

Write

9 On a piece of paper, write about where you were on your birthday last year.

On my last birthday, my friend and I were in . . .

⊙ **Extra practice**
- **Student Book, page 116, Lesson 5A**
- **Language Builder: WB, page 34; GB, page 112**
- **Student CD-ROM, Unit 5**

It chased the cat!

Grammar	Simple past of regular verbs
Vocabulary	Common regular verbs
Function	Talk about what you did

Get started

1 Look at the picture of the men and the dog. Who is the owner of the dog?

Read

2 🎧 ²⁰₅ Listen and read along. Were you right in Exercise 1?

Urban myths—true or false?

Bad dog!

A young man **arrived** for a job interview at the house of a rich businessman. On his way to the house, he **noticed** a big black dog in the man's yard. **Did** he **like** dogs? No, he **didn't**. He **hated** them. He **hurried** to the house. The dog **followed** him into the businessman's living room. It **didn't behave** well. It **walked** all over the house. It **jumped** on the sofa with its dirty paws. It **chased** the cat. The businessman **didn't stop** the dog, and he **didn't talk** to it at all. The young man was very surprised. The interview **finished** and he **walked** out of the house. The businessman **stopped** him and **called** out: "Don't forget your dog!"

Comprehension

3a Read the story again and number the pictures in the correct order.

b Do you think the story is true or false? Why?

Vocabulary: Common regular verbs

4 Read these verbs and check the meaning of any new ones.

- answer • arrive • ask • behave • call • carry
- chase • decide • discover • drop • finish
- follow • happen • hate • hurry • jump • like
- listen • look • love • notice • open • order
- pick • realize • remember • reply • start
- stay • stop • talk • taste • turn • walk
- want • watch

Grammar

Simple past of regular verbs

Affirmative	Negative
He hat**ed** dogs.	He **didn't hate** cats.
He stop**ped** the man.	He **didn't stop** the dog.
He hurr**ied** to the house.	He **didn't hurry** to the car.
Questions	**Short answers**
What **did** the dog **chase**?	A cat.
Did it **chase** a cat?	Yes, it **did**. No, it **didn't**.

☛ Go to page 132, Master your grammar.

Note

To make an affirmative simple past form, we usually add -ed or -d to the base form. For some verbs, we also double the final consonant (*stop* → *stopped*). For other verbs, we change *y* to *i* (*hurry* → *hurried*).

Practice

5 Write the simple past form of the verbs in Exercise 4 in your notebook. Be careful with the spelling of *carry*, *drop*, *hurry*, *reply*, and *stop*.

Pronunciation: -ed endings

6 🎧 Go to page 126.

7 Complete the text with the simple past form of the verbs in parentheses.

A famous blind jazz musician was on a flight across the U.S. The plane ¹ ___*stopped*___ (stop) in Chicago for 40 minutes. The pilot ² _____ (love) jazz music, so he ³ _____ (talk) to the musician.

"Is there anything we can do for you?"
⁴ _____ (ask) the pilot. "Well, yes," ⁵ _____ (answer) the musician. "My guide dog needs a walk, but I ⁶ _____ (not/want) to get off the plane. Could you walk him outside?"

The pilot ⁷ _____ (walk) the dog around the plane. When the passengers ⁸ _____ (look) out of the window, they ⁹ _____ (notice) the pilot with a guide dog. They ¹⁰ _____ (not ask) any questions. They just ¹¹ _____ (hurry) off the plane!

8 PAIRS Ask and answer questions about Exercise 7.

1 the plane/stop/in New York?
   A: *Did the plane stop in New York?*
   B: *No, it didn't.*
2 the pilot/talk to/the musician?
3 the musician/walk/the guide dog?
4 the passengers/notice/the guide dog?
5 the passengers/stay/on the plane?
6 the pilot/be/blind?

Speak

9 PAIRS Ask and answer questions. Use the cues.

1 Walk to school this morning? What time/arrive?
   A: *Did you walk to school this morning?*
   B: *Yes, I did.*
   A: *What time did you arrive?...*
2 Watch TV last night? What/watch?
3 Call a friend yesterday? Who/call?
   What/talk about?

Write

10 On a piece of paper, write a story, using the pictures and the cues below.
A girl walked into an ice cream shop in ...

girl/walk into ice cream shop

want an ice cream/order a very big one

turn around/notice Brad Pitt behind her

look at him/drop the ice cream on his shoes

 Extra practice
• Student Book, page 116, Lesson 5B
• Language Builder: WB, page 36; GB, page 113
• Student CD-ROM, Unit 5

5c I lost my bus pass!

Grammar	Simple past of irregular verbs
	Past adverbial phrases with *ago*
Vocabulary	Verb and noun collocations
Function	Make and respond to apologies

Get started

1 PAIRS Discuss these questions.

Is it OK to be late for these occasions?
a) a class   b) dinner at home
c) a date with a friend   d) a party

Presentation

2 Listen and read along. Why is Lin angry at Greg?

Comprehension

3 Match Greg's excuses in Exercise 2 to the words below.

Greg's excuses

__c__ 1 Excuse 1	a) shopping
_____ 2 Excuse 2	b) an animal
_____ 3 Excuse 3	c) a talk with a friend
_____ 4 Excuse 4	d) a problem with transportation
_____ 5 Excuse 5	e) housework

Solve it!

4 Imagine the date is Wednesday, March 26. Write the dates in each of the situations 1–5.

What happened?

1 On Monday _____ *March 24* _____
Sorry I'm late, Lin. I **left** an hour ago, but I **met** Carlos on the way here. He **told** me a long story, and I didn't notice the time.

2 Last Friday _____
I'm really sorry, Lin. I **lost** my bus pass. I think it **fell** out of my pocket. I **didn't have** any money, so I walked.

3 Yesterday morning _____
Sorry about this. I **got up** late because we **had** a party last night. Then I **made** my breakfast and **did** the dishes.

4 Three days ago _____
Believe it or not, I dropped a $5 bill in the street and a dog **ate** it! Luckily, Dad **gave** me some more money. I **came** as soon as I could.

5 Last Saturday evening _____
Sorry I'm late. I **bought** you a new calculator, but it **took** a long time to find the right one. I **went** to a lot of stores. Then I **left** the calculator in the store!

Grammar

Simple past of irregular verbs	
Affirmative	**Negative**
I **lost** my bus pass.	I **didn't lose** my train ticket.
Questions	**Short answers**
Did you **buy** a bus pass?	Yes, I **did**./ No, I **didn't**.
Past Adverbial phrases with *ago*	
I left **an hour ago**. She came **three days/weeks/months ago**.	

☛ Go to page 132, Master your grammar.

Practice

5 In your notebook, write the infinitive and past forms of each irregular verb in Exercise 2.

Infinitive	Past
leave	*left*

6 Complete with simple past forms of the verbs.

Carlos: Greg, it's seven o'clock! What happened?
1_____*Did*_____ you _____*go*_____ (you/go) to the wrong theater?

Greg: No, sorry. I 2_____ (take) a shower, and I 3_____ (leave) my watch in the bathroom.

Carlos: When 4_____ (you/leave) the house?

Greg: An hour ago. I 5_____ (do) my homework before I 6_____ (come).

Carlos: How long 7_____ (it/take you)?

Greg: About five minutes. Anyway, I 8_____ (not/come) straight here. I 9_____ (go) to see Lin first. I 10_____ (lose) her calculator last week, so I 11_____ (buy) another one.

Carlos: OK. Come on. The movie is starting.

Speak

7 PAIRS Make sentences that are true for you. Use the words in the box.

Last summer I went to Los Angeles.

- Last summer   • Last week   • Two days ago
- Last night   • This morning

Vocabulary: Verb and noun collocations

8 Match the verbs to the correct nouns.

_*e*_	1 make	a)	a story, a lie, the truth
_____	2 do	b)	a party, a snack, dinner
_____	3 lose	c)	the dishes, homework
_____	4 miss	d)	a ticket, some money
_____	5 tell	e)	sandwiches, a cake, lunch
_____	6 have	f)	the bus, the train

Use your English: Make and respond to apologies

9 PAIRS Listen and repeat. Then practice the conversation.

A: I'm sorry I'm late.
B: What happened?
A: I took the wrong bus!
B: Never mind. You're here now.

Apologize for being late
• Sorry I'm late.

Accept
• That's OK./all right.   • What happened?

Explain
• (Believe it or not), I took the wrong bus.

Respond
• It doesn't matter.   • Never mind.
• Don't worry.   • Not again!

10 PAIRS Practice conversations. Use the cues.

- fall off/my bike   • lose/your address
- miss/the train   • go/to the wrong house

Write

11 On a piece of paper, write a paragraph about a situation when you apologized to someone for something you did.

Last week, I was late for school. I got up at . . .

> ## Extra practice
> - **Student Book, page 117, Lesson 5C**
> - **Language Builder: WB, page 38; GB, page 113**
> - **Student CD-ROM, Unit 5**

INTEGRATED CONSOLIDATION SKILLS

Curriculum link: History

"Gold! Gold from the American River!"

Who found the first gold?

Before 1848, the state of California in the U.S. was a very quiet place. The population was just 20,000 people. Then, on January 24, 1848, a man called James Marshall saw something shiny in a river in a place called Sutter's Fort. He showed his friends. "Boys," he said, "I think this is gold!"

How did the gold rush start?

A man called Sam Brennan started it. He heard about the gold and opened a new store near Sutter's Fort. He wanted to sell the tools that people needed to look for gold. He needed a gold rush. In May 1848, he filled a bottle with gold dust and ran through the streets of San Francisco shouting "Gold! Gold! Gold from the American River!"

Did Brennan's plan work?

Yes, it did. Everyone in San Francisco left their jobs and became gold diggers. San Francisco was almost empty. Schools closed because there weren't any teachers. In August 1848, the governor of California sent some gold to the president of the U.S. When the people of New York saw the gold, the gold rush really began. By 1850 the population of California was 100,000. Some men found a lot of gold, but others weren't so lucky.

What happened to James Marshall and Sam Brennan?

One man became a millionaire and the other man didn't. Can you guess who became a millionaire?

Get started

1 Imagine you find gold in a river. What do you do?

a) You take it home and don't tell anyone.

b) You only tell your friends.

c) You tell everyone.

Read

Learning strategy: Scan for specific information
When you scan a text, don't read from start to finish. Just look for the information you want (a name, a date).

2 Read the article above. Who are the four people in this story?

_____

_____

New words and phrases
- gold rush • population • see (saw) • shiny
- show(ed) • hear (heard) • store • sell (sold)
- tool • fill(ed) • dust • run (ran) • through
- shout(ed) • became • gold digger • empty
- close(d) • governor • send (sent) • president
- begin (began) • find (found) • millionaire

Comprehension

3 Number the events in the correct order.

_____ a) People left their jobs to go and find gold.

_____ b) The governor sent gold to the president.

_1_ c) Marshall found gold in the river.

_____ d) People from New York joined the gold rush.

_____ e) Brennan opened a new store.

_____ f) Marshall told his friends about the gold.

4 Answer the questions. Scan the text.

When . . .

1 did Marshall discover the first gold?
_____ _1848_ _____

2 did Brennan put gold dust in a bottle?
_____

3 did the governor send gold to the president?
_____

Where . . .

4 did Marshall discover gold? _____
5 was Brennan's store? _____

Listen

5a Listen. Which man became a millionaire: Marshall or Brennan? _____

Marshall

Brennan

b Listen again. Correct the mistakes.

few
1 A ~~lot of~~ gold diggers became rich.

2 Levi Strauss sold water for $100 a glass.

3 Chinese people opened clothing stores.

4 California gold diggers smelled good.

Speak

6a PAIRS Read the conversation and write five more lines in your notebook. Then act it out.

Hello. My name's Levi Strauss. I think you need a new pair of pants. Look at these.

What are they?

b Now look at the cartoon below and act out the conversation.

WATER $100 A GLASS

Write

7 You are a gold digger in California in 1849. You find gold. Answer the questions. Then write your diary entry for that day on a piece of paper.

1 Did you feel lucky this morning? _____
2 What did you have for breakfast? _____
3 What time did you find gold? _____
4 Where did you find gold? _____
5 Were you alone? _____
6 What did you do next? _____
7 What's the first thing you bought? _____

Monday, May 20, 1849

When I woke up this morning, I felt very lucky. I had beans and coffee for breakfast. At first I didn't find any gold, but then at about . . .

CLIL PROJECT, page 140

Was she driving?

Grammar	Past continuous
Vocabulary	The weather
Function	Talk about ongoing activities in the past

Get started

1 April 1 is April Fool's Day. What do people do on this day?

Presentation

2 🎧 2 10 **Listen and read along. Who did Greg and Carlos say they met?**

Greg: Guess who we met yesterday? Her!

Polly: Who? Shakira! Where?

Carlos: Outside the school at around 3 P.M. We **were walking** home.

Polly: What **was** she **doing**?

Greg: She **was sitting** in a white limo.

Polly: **Was** she **driving**?

Carlos: No, she **wasn't**. She was in the back. Anyway, it **was raining**, so Greg said, "Hi, Shakira. Can you give us a ride home?"

Polly: No way! Did she give you a ride?

Greg: I wish! No, she didn't, but she gave us two tickets for her next concert.

Polly: Are you serious? Let me see. Hey, these are old movie tickets!

Carlos: April Fool!

Comprehension

3 Answer the questions about Greg's story.

1 Where did the boys see the woman? _outside school_

2 What kind of car was she in? _____

3 What was the weather like? _____

4 What did Greg ask the woman? _____

5 What did she give them? _____

6 Was the story true? _____

💡 Solve it!

4 Today is Monday, April 1. What day is Shakira's next concert?

48

Grammar

Past continuous	
Affirmative	**Negative**
At 3 P.M. yesterday . . .	
She **was sitting**.	She **wasn't driving**.
We **were walking** home.	We **weren't shopping**.
Questions	**Short answers**
Was she **driving**?	Yes, she **was**./No, she **wasn't**.
Were you **going** home?	Yes, I **was**./No, I **wasn't**.
What were you **doing**?	I **was shopping**.

☞ Go to page 133, Master your grammar.

Practice

5 PAIRS Look at the photo in Exercise 2. Ask and answer questions. Imagine it was yesterday.

1 What/Greg/wear? (a T-shirt and jeans)

A: *What was Greg wearing?*

B: *He was wearing a T-shirt and jeans.*

2 Where/the three friends? (at a bus stop)

3 What/the man/do? (look at the bus schedule)

4 What/the woman/do? (walk her dog)

6 PAIRS Look at Greg's plans for last Saturday. Ask and answer questions about what Greg was doing at these times.

1) A: *What was he doing at 9:15 on Saturday?*

B: *He was cleaning his room.*

2) 10:00 A.M.   3) 12:45 P.M.   4) 3:00 P.M.

5) 6:20 P.M.   6)   9:00 P.M.

> *Saturday—things to do!*
> *9:00-9:30 a.m.   clean my room*
> *9:30-11:30 a.m.   do my homework*
> *12:30-1:00 p.m.   call Polly*
> *2:00-4:00 p.m.   play basketball*
> *6:00-6:30 p.m.   have dinner*
> *8:00-10:00 p.m.   watch TV*

Speak

7 PAIRS Ask and answer about last Saturday. Use the times in Exercise 6.

A: *What were you doing at a quarter past nine?*

B: *I was sleeping/having breakfast.*

Pronunciation: /ɑ/ hot, /ɔr/ bored

8 🎧 Go to page 126.

Vocabulary: The weather

9 Review. What is the weather like in the pictures? Say other weather words you know. Then check the Word bank on page 125.

Listen

10 🎧 ²/₁₄ Listen to Sarah's story. Correct the mistakes.

1 The afternoon was ~~warm~~. *cold*

2 It was getting light.

3 Sarah was riding a bus.

4 A woman was listening to music.

5 The woman asked about Sarah's cell phone.

Write

11 On a piece of paper, describe the weather. Use these questions for ideas.

• What was the weather like yesterday?

• Where were you?

• How were you feeling at the time?

• What were you doing?

> **Extra practice**
> • Student Book, page 117, Lesson 6A
> • Language Builder: WB, page 42; GB, page 116
> • Student CD-ROM, Unit 6

Grammar	Past continuous and simple past with *while* and *when*
Vocabulary	Prepositions of location and motion
Function	Tell stories

Get started

1 Look at the pictures. What is happening in them?

Read

2 🔊 2/15 Listen and read along. Then choose the best title for each story. Write it above the story.

a) *Dangerous Driver*   b) *Great Minds Think Alike*

Comprehension

3 Answer the questions. Complete the chart.

Who . . .	Herman	Vincent	Michael
1 broke into a house?	✔	✔	
2 was in a car?			
3 waited in the bedroom?			
4 liked a beautiful woman?			
5 was in a wardrobe?			
6 kidnapped the wrong person?			

Grammar

Past continuous and simple past with *while* and *when*

While Herman **was waiting**, another man jumped out.

Herman was waiting **when** another man **jumped out**.

☛ Go to page 133, Master your grammar.

Practice

4 Match cues from A with cues from B. Then, in your notebook, write sentences with *when*.

1 – c) She was swimming when she saw a shark.

A
1 she (swim)
2 they (have) a party
3 he (do) homework
4 I (watch) a movie
5 she (drive) a car

B
a) their parents (come) home
b) my phone rang
c) she (see) a shark
d) she (hit) a tree
e) he (fall) asleep

Crazy crimes

1 _____

A man named Herman decided to kidnap a rich businessman. He broke into the businessman's house, went into the bedroom, and waited. **While** Herman **was waiting**, another man, Vincent, **jumped** out of the dresser and kidnapped Herman. Vincent was a kidnapper, too. He thought Herman was the businessman. Vincent locked Herman in the house for two days. Finally, Vincent realized his mistake.

2 _____

A man named Michael Todd **was driving** past a railway station **when** he **saw** a beautiful woman. **While** she **was buying a ticket**, he **shouted** hello. She didn't reply, so he followed her into the station—in his car. He drove through the station entrance, past the ticket office, and up the steps. Then he drove along the platform and stopped next to the woman. He **was** still **sitting** in his car **when** police **arrested** him.

5 In your notebook, write sentences with *while* and *when* for each set of cues.

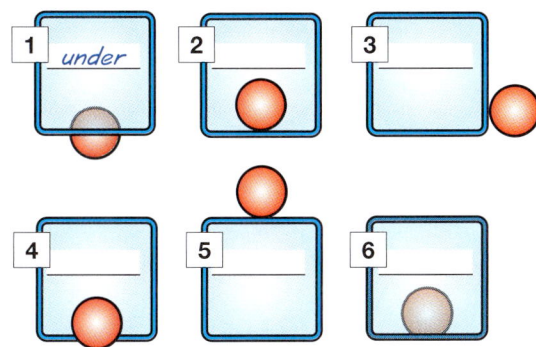

Steven Bickley, the world's worst burglar

1 Steven/drive his car/see/an open window
  a While Steven was driving his car, he . . .
  b Steven was driving his car when he saw . . .
2 no one look/he climb/a ladder/and break into the house
3 he/take things from the house/see some food in the kitchen
4 he/watch TV in the house/fall asleep
5 he sleep/house owner come back/and call the police

Vocabulary: Prepositions of location and motion

6a Review. Write prepositions of location in the diagrams. Then check the Word bank on page 125.

1 *under*	2	3

4	5	6

b Extension. Listen and repeat the prepositions of motion.

• across • along • down • into • out of
• over • past • through • up

Speak

7 PAIRS Look at the pictures. Take turns saying what Steven Bickley did. Use the cues and prepositions of motion.

1 *He jumped over a wall.*

1 jump/wall

2 climb/ladder

3 climb/window

4 walk/room

5 walk/stairs

6 go/kitchen

Write

8 On a piece of paper, write the story of Steven Bickley. Use the information in Exercises 5 and 7.

Steven Bickley is the world's worst burglar. Last week, while he was driving his car, he saw . . .

> **Extra practice**
> • Student Book, page 118, Lesson 6B
> • Language Builder: WB, page 44; GB, page 117
> • Student CD-ROM, Unit 6

A monster that comes alive

Grammar	Adjective clauses with *who*, *that*, and *where*
Vocabulary	Types of movies
Function	Buy tickets at the theater

1 *The Twilight Saga: Eclipse*

2 *Shrek Forever After*

Get started

1 What was your favorite movie this year? Why?

Vocabulary: Types of movies

2a Listen and repeat. Then match the photos to the types of movies.

___ an action movie ___ an animated movie ___ a comedy ___ a crime movie
___ a fantasy movie ___ a horror movie ___ a musical *1* a romance
___ a science fiction movie ___ a spy movie ___ a thriller ___ a western

3 *Avatar*

b Look at the types of movies that are not in the photos. Think of a movie title for each type of movie.

4 *Grown Ups*

Presentation

3 Listen and read along. Who buys the tickets?

Polly: *The Karate Kid* is sold out. Which movie do you want to see instead?

Lin: How about *Girl of My Dreams*? It's about a young man **who** dreams about the perfect girl. The next day he goes to a bookstore, **where** he meets her.

Greg: That's a romance! No, thank you!

Carlos: What about *Journey into Space*? It's about some astronauts **who** go to Mars.

Lin: Hmm. It doesn't sound very exciting. Is there anything else playing?

Polly: How about *The Pyramid*? It's a horror movie about a monster in an Egyptian pyramid **that** comes alive.

Greg: OK, that's better. Should I get the tickets?

Polly: Yes, but let's hurry. It's 5:30. The next showing starts in five minutes.

BOX OFFICE

Comprehension

4 Answer the questions.

1 Which movies do the friends suggest that they see?
2 What types of movies are they?
3 Which movie do they agree to see?

💡 Solve it!

5 What time does the movie start?

Grammar

Adjective clauses with *who*, *that*, and *where*

People (*who* or *that*)

It's about astronauts **who/that** go to Mars.

Things

It's about a monster **that** comes alive.

Places

He goes to a bookstore, **where** he meets a girl.

☛ Go to page 133, Master your grammar.

Practice

6 Complete with *who*, *that*, or *where*.

1 I live in a town ___where___ there aren't any theaters.
2 I saw a boy _____ looked like Harry Potter!
3 I don't like movies _____ have talking animals.
4 Do you know a store _____ I can buy DVDs?
5 Is that the actor _____ was in *Star Wars*?
6 I have book _____ has photos of Mars.

7 In your notebook, rewrite the story of *The Karate Kid* with *who*, *that*, or *where*.

1 *Dre and his mother move to China, where his mother has a new job.*

The Karate Kid

1 Dre and his mother move to China. In China, his mother has a new job.

2 Dre goes to a new school. At the school, other boys bully and hit him.

3 Dre meets Mr. Han. Mr. Han is very good at martial arts.

4 Mr. Han gives Dre martial arts training. The training teaches him special new skills.

5 Dre signs up for a contest. At the contest, he fights the bullies and wins.

Speak

8 PAIRS Ask and answer the questions.

1 What was the last movie you saw?
2 What was it about?

Use your English: Buy tickets at the theater

9 PAIRS Listen and repeat. Then practice the conversation.

A: Can I have four tickets for *Avatar*, please?
B: Which showing? The 5:00 or the 7:30?
A: The 5:00, please. How much is that?
B: That's $40, please.

Ask for tickets
• Hello. I'd like/Can I have four adult ticket(s) for *Avatar*, please?

Ask about the performance
• Which showing? The 5:00 or the 7:30?

Say the showing
• The 5:00 showing, please.

Ask the price
• How much is that?

Give the price
• That's $40, please.

10 PAIRS Practice similar conversations. Use the movie schedule.

Odeon Multiplex Theater

Avatar	2:30	5:00	7:30
The Twilight Saga: Eclipse	5:15	8:00	
Shrek Forever After	2:45	6:30	8:00
The Karate Kid	5:30	7:15	
Tickets: $10			

Write

11 On a piece of paper, write the story of a movie. Use your sentences from Exercise 7 as a model. Use *who*, *that*, and *where*.

> **Extra practice**
> • Student Book, page 118, Lesson 6C
> • Language Builder: WB, page 46; GB, page 118
> • Student CD-ROM, Unit 6

INTEGRATED SKILLS **CONSOLIDATION**

Values for living

Get started

1 What do you say in this situation?
Choose the best response: a), b), or c).

> You and your friend are going to catch a bus.
> Your friend says, "Don't buy a ticket. They
> never check."

a) "OK."   b) "Are you sure?"   c) "No."

Read

2 Read the story. How did Kayla's friend get
into the festival? _____

Comprehension

3 Complete the sentences about the story.

1 The music festival is going to be _in the park_.
2 They _____ buy tickets.
3 On Wednesday, they arranged to _____.
4 Oscar went into the festival under _____.
5 Kayla didn't go into the festival because _____
_____.

Speak your mind!

> **Learning strategy: Prepare before
> speaking**
>
> Before you do a speaking task, make a list
> of things you want to say and practice in
> your head.

4a Should Kayla go under the fence? Make
two lists of reasons in your notebook.

Reasons to go   *Reasons not to go*
Oscar is going in.   *She doesn't have a ticket.*

b Imagine you are Kayla. What are you going
to do and why?

*I'm going to go under the fence and into the
festival because it's going to be fun. I can't buy
a ticket, so . . .*

Going under the fence

Kayla James is a student at a high school in California. Oscar is a good friend.

On Wednesday, Oscar called Kayla.
"Hey, do you know about the music festival in the park on Saturday? Tons of bands are going to be there, including The Jonas Brothers."
"The Jonas Brothers!" Kayla said. "They're my favorite band."
"I know," Oscar said, "but there aren't any tickets. They sold out yesterday."
"So I guess we can't go," said Kayla. "What about going to the movies instead?"
"Hmm . . . yes, OK," said Oscar.

Three days later, Kayla met Oscar outside the theater.

"What movie do you want to see?" Kayla asked.
"We're not going to see a movie," Oscar said with a smile. He had a piece of paper in his hand. "We're going to the music festival."
"Do you have tickets?" Kayla asked. She was surprised.
"No, I don't," Oscar said, "but I have a map that is going to help us to get in."
Half an hour later they were standing next to a fence outside the festival. Five of Oscar's friends

Listen

> **Listening tip: Focus your listening**
> Before you listen, read the questions carefully.
> Then listen for that information.

5 Listen. Answer the questions in your notebook.

1 Where can they sit in the festival? *in cafés*
2 Why doesn't Kayla want to go under the fence?
3 Does Oscar think it's wrong to go under the fence?
4 Why is Kayla angry?
5 Does Kayla go under the fence?

Speak

6 PAIRS What do you think? Does Kayla make the right choice? Why?

Write

7 Look at the picture. It shows an alternative ending to the story. Write the alternative ending on a piece of paper.

While no one was looking, Kayla went under the fence. But a security guard saw her . . .

Her parents were waiting for her.

were there, too. Then, when no one was looking, they crawled under the fence and into the festival. Then it was Oscar and Kayla's turn. "Do you want to go first?" Oscar asked. "No, you go," Kayla said. Oscar crawled under the fence and disappeared into the festival. Kayla didn't move. Was this a good idea? She wasn't sure. It was starting to rain and she was getting wet. She didn't know what to do.

> **New words and phrases**
> • tons of • including • smile (*n*)
> • piece of paper • surprised • crawl(ed)
> • turn (*n*) • disappear(ed) • get wet

CLIL PROJECT, page 140

Review: Units 5 & 6

Grammar (40 points)

1 Complete with past forms. (10 points)

Mom: How ⁰ _____was_____ (be) the movie last night?

Greg: Excellent, thanks.

Mom: You ¹ _____ (come) home late. What ² _____ (happen)?

Greg: I'm sorry. I ³ _____ (miss) the last bus. The movie ⁴ _____ (not end) until 10:45. I ⁵ _____ (call) for a taxi, but then I ⁶ _____ (look) in my wallet. There ⁷ _____ (be) no money in it!

Mom: ⁸ _____ (walk) home?

Greg: Yes, I ⁹ _____ (do). It ¹⁰ _____ (not be) much fun!

2 Complete with the correct past tense form of a verb from the box. (10 points)

> • be • buy • come • do • eat • ~~get up~~
> • give • go • meet • take • tell

Yesterday I ⁰ _____got up_____ at 9:30. I ¹ _____ a shower. Then I ² _____ some breakfast and ³ _____ the dishes. At 11 A.M., I ⁴ _____ to the store and ⁵ _____ a magazine. Sam ⁶ _____ into the store. I ⁷ _____ his cousin Lisa. She ⁸ _____ cute! Sam ⁹ _____ me about his vacation. Lisa ¹⁰ _____ me her cell phone number.

3 Write past questions and answers. (6 points)

0 What time/you/wake up today? (7:30)

A: *What time did you wake up today?*

B: *I woke up at 7:30.*

1 What/you/have/for breakfast? (eggs)

A: _____

B: _____

2 he/do/his homework last night? (Yes/all of it)

A: _____

B: _____

3 How/you/get to school today? (go by bus)

A: _____

B: _____

4 my parents/call? (Yes, at 4 P.M.)

A: _____

B: _____

5 When/she/buy her bike? (three months ago)

A: _____

B: _____

6 she/make you lunch? (Yes/some pasta)

A: _____

B: _____

4 Write sentences with *when* or *while* and the past continuous or simple past. (7 points)

0 He/have an accident/walk home (while)

He had an accident while he was walking home.

00 I/talk to Ana/drop the phone (when)

I was talking to Ana when I dropped the phone.

1 She/fall asleep/do her homework (while)

_____

2 I/get up/our friends arrive (when)

_____

3 They/stay/in Kenya/see elephants (while)

_____

4 We/take our dog for a walk/start to rain (when)

_____

5 They/stay in Miami/go to the beach (while)

_____

6 She/watch a DVD/her mom call (when)

_____

7 She/shop in town/lose her purse (while)

_____

5 Complete the sentences with *who, that,* or *where*. (7 points)

0 This is the town _____where_____ I lived when I was five.

1 Is there a store near here _____ sells computers?

2 Can we find a place _____ we can sit down?

3 I don't like people _____ smoke in the street.

4 Students _____ are late get extra homework.

5 What is a girl's name _____ begins with S?

6 I went to a school _____ I learned Chinese.

7 Is she the actress _____ played Elizabeth I?

Vocabulary (40 points)

6 Write the dates. Put them in order. (12 points)

> • Dec 12 • June 4 • Mar 9 • ~~Jan 2~~ • Aug 18
> • Jul 15 • Sept 10 • Feb 21 • Nov 30 • Apr 3
> • Oct 5 • May 31 • Jan 14

0 *January second,* _____

_____

_____

_____

7 Complete each sentence with a verb and a phrase from the box. (5 points)

> • bus • dishes • key • lie • lunch • party

0 Don't _miss_ the _bus_. They only go every hour.
1 That's not true. Don't _____ a _____.
2 Lock the door and please don't _____ the _____!
3 Look at these dirty plates. Can you ____ the ____?
4 What time do you usually _____ _____ at school?
5 Let's _____ a _____ for Tim's birthday!

8 Write what the weather is like. (7 points)

0 _It's_
  sunny.
1 _____
  _____
2 _____
  _____
3 _____
  _____
4 _____
  _____
5 _____
  _____
6 _____
  _____
7 _____
  _____

30°F
100°F

9 Write the correct preposition. (8 points)

> • across • along • down • into • out of
> • over • through • under • up

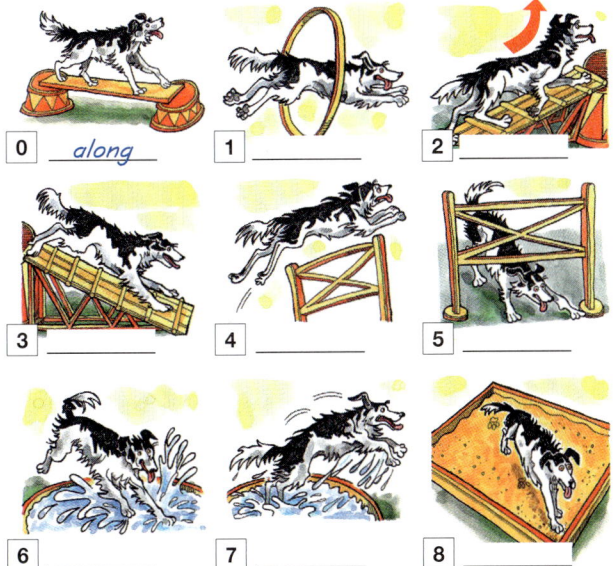

0 _along_
1 _____
2 _____
3 _____
4 _____
5 _____
6 _____
7 _____
8 _____

10 Complete the movie words with syllables from the box. (8 points)

> • ance • cal • edy • ler • mated • ror
> • tasy • tern • toon

0 ani_mated_   1 car_____   2 com_____
3 musi_____   4 wes_____   5 fan_____
6 rom_____   7 thril_____ 8 hor_____

Use your English (20 points)

11 Choose the correct response. (10 points)

0 **A:** What's Beyoncé's last name?
  B: a) (Dunno.) b) Cool!
1 **A:** I'm getting up at five o'clock tomorrow.
  B: a) Of course not! b) You're crazy!
2 **A:** Can I have some cake?
  B: a) Yes, of course. b) I'm back!
3 **A:** We have a math test tomorrow.
  B: a) Are you serious? b) I wish!
4 **A:** Did you take my cell phone?
  B: a) Cool! b) Of course not!
5 **A:** Wow! Are those tickets for the rock concert?
  B: a) I wish! b) I'm back!

12 Complete the conversation with words from the box. (10 points)

> • all • Believe • Can • for • mind • much
> • or • Sorry • That's • What • Which

A: 0 _Sorry_ I'm late.
B: That's 1 _____ right. 2 _____ happened?
A: 3 _____ it or not, I missed the bus.
B: Never 4 _____ ! Let's get the tickets.
A: OK. 5 _____ we have two tickets
   6 _____ *Toy Story 3*?
C: 7 _____ showing? The 5:40
   8 _____ the 7:20?
A: The 7:20, please. How 9 _____ is that?
C: 10 _____ $20, please.

SELF-CHECK	
Grammar	_____ /40
Vocabulary	_____ /40
Use your English	_____ /20
Total score	_____ /100

It's too noisy.

Grammar	*too* + adjective (+ infinitive)
	(not) + adjective + *enough*
	(+ infinitive)
Vocabulary	Places in town
Function	Talk about problems in your town

Get started

1 Do you live in the city or the country? Which is better? Why?

Read

2 🎧 Listen and read along. Where do Leroy and Caitlin live? _____

Comprehension

3 Answer the questions.

1 What does Leroy like about New York?
2 What doesn't he like about the country?
3 What does Caitlin like doing in the summer?
4 What does she like doing in the winter?
5 What doesn't she like about the city?

City life or *country life?*

Which place is better—the city or the country? Two American teenagers talk about where they live.

I live in New York and it's great. There are huge buildings and interesting places to go. My mom loves all the art galleries and museums, but I like Central Park, where I go skateboarding. It's **big enough to get** away from the noise and the traffic. The country isn't for me. It is**n't exciting enough** for people my age. Most people do**n't** live **close enough** to their friends **to have** a good social life. It's **too quiet** and **too boring**. City life rules!

Leroy, 16

I live on a ranch in the country, in Colorado. In the summer we go hiking in the mountains, and in the winter I go snowboarding. I really like it because it's relaxing and quiet. I can't imagine life in the city. It is**n't safe enough to walk** around alone, and it's **too dangerous to ride** your bike on the streets because of the traffic. Overall I think the city is **too noisy**, **too dirty**, **too crowded**, and **too expensive**. I prefer country life!

Caitlin, 14

Vocabulary: Places in town

4a Review. In your notebook, list places in town. Then check the Word bank on page 125.

b 🎧 2/22 Extension. Listen and repeat. Then match the words in the box to the symbols. Which words don't have a symbol?

> • gas station • hospital • hotel • library
> • market • museum • police station
> • shopping mall • ~~theater~~
> • tourist information center • town hall • zoo

1 *theater*
2 _____
3 _____
4 _____
5 _____
6 _____
7 _____
8 _____

5 PAIRS Talk about places in your town.

There's a shopping center next to the library.

Grammar

too + adjective	*not* + adjective + *enough*
The country is **too quiet**.	The country is**n't** **exciting enough**.
too + adjective + infinitive	*not* + adjective + *enough* + infinitive
The city's **too dangerous to ride** your bike.	The city's **not safe enough to walk** around alone.

☛ Go to page 134, Master your grammar.

Practice

6 Read the survey notes. In your notebook, write sentences with *too* or *not . . . enough.*

The center of town isn't exciting enough.

> ### What's wrong with your town?
> 1 The center of town/not/exciting
> 2 The shopping mall/crowded
> 3 The library/small
> 4 The supermarket parking lot/not/big
> 5 The theater/expensive
> 6 The zoo/far from the town center
> 7 The museum/not/interesting

7 In your notebook, combine the sentences with *too . . . to* or *(not) . . . enough . . . to.*

1 It's far to the theater. We can't walk there.
   It's too far to walk to the theater.
2 This zoo isn't big. It doesn't have any lions or tigers.
3 It's very early. We can't go to the museum.
4 The library isn't modern. It doesn't have computers.
5 The lake is warm. You can swim in it.
6 The stores are expensive. We can't buy anything there.

Speak

8 PAIRS Talk about problems in your town.

Our theater isn't big enough.

Write

9 On a piece of paper, write about your town. Use the questions to help you.

- Where do you live?
- What is there in your town?
- What do you do in the summer/winter?
- Do you like your town? Why?/Why not?

> ### ❯ Extra practice
> - **Student Book, page 119, Lesson 7A**
> - **Language Builder: WB, page 50; GB, page 120**
> - **Student CD-ROM, Unit 7**

How long is he staying?

Grammar	Present continuous for future plans
Vocabulary	Transportation
Function	Talk about travel plans

Get started

1 Look at the photo. Where are the friends?

Presentation

2 🎧 2 23 Listen and read along. Who are the friends waiting for?

Lin: I can't wait to see Jiang again.

Greg: Remind me. Who's Jiang? Is he your cousin?

Lin: No, he isn't. He's a family friend. He's from Hong Kong, but he works in New York.

Polly: Is he good-looking?

Lin: Hmm, not bad, but he's a little old for you!

Greg: How long **is** he **staying**?

Lin: About ten days. He's **taking** my mom and me to San Francisco next weekend.

Polly: That's a long way. **Are** you **going** by car?

Lin: No, we aren't. We're **going** by plane. He's **treating** us!

Polly: He sounds great!

Greg: Yeah, great.

Lin: Oh, Greg, you're jealous.

Greg: Me, jealous? Come on! Hey, we have half an hour before his train arrives at 3 P.M. Let's get a soda. It's my treat!

Comprehension

3 Complete the details about Jiang.

Name:	Jiang Feng
From:	[1] *Hong Kong,*
Relation to Lin:	[2] _____
Is from:	[3] _____
Job in:	[4] _____
Time in Seattle:	[5] _____ days
Weekend plans:	[6] _____

 Solve it!

4 Look at the conversation on page 60. What time does Jiang's train arrive?

Grammar

Present continuous for future plans

How long **is** he **staying**?
Are you **going** by car?
No, we **aren't**. We**'re going** by plane.

☛ Go to page 134, Master your grammar.

Practice

5 Complete the conversation. Use the correct form of the present continuous.

Greg: [1] *What are you doing* (what/do) on Saturday?

Lin: [2] _____ (I/meet/Polly) in town in the morning.

Greg: [3] _____? (you/go shop?)

Lin: [4] _____. (Yes)

Greg: And [5] _____ (what/you/do) in the afternoon?

Lin: [6] _____ (We/go) to a party.

Greg: But [7] _____ (I/have) a party at my house.

Lin: Remind me. [8] _____ (Why/you/have) a party?

Greg: Because it's my birthday! [9] _____. (Whose party/you/go to?)

Lin: Yours, silly. [10] _____ (Polly and I/go shop) for your present in the morning!

Vocabulary: Transportation

6a **Review.** How many forms of transportation can you think of? Write them in your notebook. Then check the Word bank on page 125.

b 🔊 2/25 **Extension.** Listen and repeat. Then match the words in the box to the pictures.

> • ~~ferry~~ • helicopter • moped • ship • trailer • van

1 *ferry*   2 _____   3 _____

4 _____   5 _____   6 _____

Speak

7 **PAIRS** Talk about travel plans. Use the cues.

A: *Where are you going?*
B: *I'm going to a hotel in Vancouver.*
A: *How are you getting there?*
B: *I'm going by bus and then ferry.*

Where to?	How	
1 A hotel in Vancouver	🚌	⛴
2 My aunt's house in Mexico	✈	🚆
3 Home	🚆	🚗

Write

8 On a piece of paper, write a paragraph about a trip you are taking soon.

I'm going to the beach soon. I'm going by bus and . . .

 Extra practice
- **Student Book, page 119, Lesson 7B**
- **Language Builder: WB, page 52; GB, page 121**
- **Student CD-ROM, Unit 7**

Grammar	*like* and *would like*
Vocabulary	Restaurant food
Function	Order food in a restaurant

Get started

1 What is your favorite restaurant? What do you eat there?

Vocabulary: Restaurant food

2a Write the headings on the menu.

> • Drinks • Fish • Desserts • Pasta
> • Side orders • ~~Meat~~

Garden Bistro Menu

1 ___Meat___
- roast beef $10.75
- roast chicken $10.50
- steak $10.95
- steak tartare $10.75
- pork chop $9.50

2 _____
- fish soup $7.25
- garlic shrimp....................... $7.25
- baked salmon $9.50

3 _____
- spaghetti bolognese $8.25
- lasagna.................................... $8.75
- ravioli..................................... $7.50

4 _____ (*all at $3.50*)
- garlic bread • baked potato
- mashed potatoes • french fries • rice
- fresh vegetables • green salad

5 _____ (*all at $5.95*)
- fruit salad • apple pie with ice cream
- vanilla ice cream • chocolate ice cream
- cheesecake • fresh fruit

6 _____ (*all at $2.50*)
- mineral water • cola • lemonade
- fruit juice • tea • coffee
- decaffeinated coffee

Note: The restaurant adds a $2 cover charge to all meals.

b Label the pictures with the words on the menu.

A	*garlic bread*	B	_____

C	_____	D	_____

E	_____	F	_____

Pronunciation: /tʃ/ <u>ch</u>eese, /ʃ/ fi<u>sh</u>

3 🎧 Go to page 127.

Grammar

> ***like* and *would like***
>
> *like*
>
> I **like** lasagna. (I think it's delicious)
> I **don't like** garlic.
>
> *would like*
>
> I**'d like** lasagna. (Can I have some?)
> **Would** you **like** some garlic bread?

☛ Go to page 134, Master your grammar.

Practice

4 PAIRS Ask and answer about the foods.

> • ~~french fries~~ • mashed potatoes
> • fish • steak • green salad

A: *Do you like french fries?*
B: *Yes, I do. I love them./No, I don't. Not very much.*
A: *Would you like some fries now?*
B: *Yes, please./No, thanks.*

Presentation

5  Listen and read along. What's wrong with Greg's food?

Waiter: **What would you like?**

Toby: **I'd like** lasagna, please.

Waiter: **Would you like some** garlic bread?

Toby: No, thanks. I don't like garlic.

Waiter: And for you?

Greg: **I'll have** the steak tartare, please.

Toby: Do you know what steak tartare is, Greg?

Greg: Yes, of course. And french fries, please.

Toby: And can we have two colas, please?

Ten minutes later:

Waiter: One lasagna and one steak tartare.

Greg: Thank you. Um . . . Toby! This isn't cooked! You didn't tell me that steak tartare is raw!

Comprehension

6 Read the conversation and complete the chart.

	Toby	Greg
Main course (meat, fish, pasta)	*lasagna*	
Side order		
Drink		
Dessert		

Listen

7 Listen to the conversation. Complete the Dessert section in Exercise 6.

💡 Solve it!

8 Look at the menu in Exercise 2a. How much does Toby and Greg's meal cost?

Use your English: Order food in a restaurant

9 Read the phrases below.

Ask what people want
- Are you ready to order?
- What would you like?
- What would you like to drink?
- Anything else?

Say what you want
- I'd like spaghetti, please.
- Lasagna for me, please.
- I'll have a steak, please.
- Can I/we have a soda, please?
- Me too, please.

Offer food or drink
- Would you like a salad?
- With french fries?

Accept or refuse
- Yes, please./No, thank you.
- Not for me, thanks.
- No. That's fine, thanks.

Ask for the check
- Can I have the check, please?

10 GROUPS Role-play conversations in a restaurant. Use the phrases above and the menu in Exercise 2a.

Write

11 On a piece of paper, write a menu for a restaurant. Use the menu in Exercise 2a as a model. Then write about what you'd like to order at the restaurant.

I'd like a hamburger and french fries . . .

> **Extra practice**
> - **Student Book, page 119, Lesson 7C**
> - **Language Builder: WB, page 54; GB, page 122**
> - **Student CD-ROM, Unit 7**

INTEGRATED CONSOLIDATION SKILLS

Across cultures

Before you read, go to page 65.

The Rainforest Café

The Hard Rock Café

New York and London are famous for their interesting restaurants. We asked Ralph, 15, from New York, and Meredith, 14, from London, and to tell us how often they eat out and where they like to go in their city.

Ralph

I eat out a lot. Once a week I go to a pizza restaurant with my friends, and twice a week I go out with my parents. We usually have a Chinese or an Italian meal. But my favorite place to eat is the Hard Rock Café. It has loud music and fantastic photos of rock singers on the walls.

Meredith

I eat out once a week. My parents usually take me to a Chinese or an Indian restaurant on the weekend. But my favorite place is the Rainforest Café in central London. It looks like a rainforest with wild animals (they're not real!), and the food's great.

Factfile

Restaurants
Italian and Chinese restaurants are popular in both New York and London. There are also a lot of Indian and Thai restaurants in London and South American restaurants in New York.

Cafés (Coffee shops)
New York has "diners." These are typical American cafés with a wide variety of foods and a long counter. London has cheap cafés where the food is fried and not very healthy. Some people call these "greasy spoon" cafés.

Where teenagers go
A survey of 13- to 16-year-old teenagers in New York and London found that:
• 85% regularly go to either burger or pizza restaurants.
• 80% say that their favorite place to celebrate a birthday is a theme restaurant such as a music café or a sports café.

New words and phrases
• rainforest • wild • eat out • fried
• greasy spoon • diner • typical • variety
• counter • celebrate • theme

Get started

1 Would you like to eat out in New York or in London? Why?

Read

2 Read the article on page 64. Which restaurant has wild animals? _____

Comprehension

3a Choose the correct answer.

1 Ralph eats out _____ a week.
  a) three times b) twice c) once
2 Ralph likes _____ in the restaurant.
  a) the food b) the music c) the people
3 Meredith sometimes eats in _____ restaurant.
  a) a Chinese b) a Thai c) an Italian
4 Meredith's favorite restaurant is _____ restaurant.
  a) an Indian b) a theme c) a fast-food

b Write *NY* (New York), *L* (London) or *NY/L* (both).

NY/L 1 There are many Italian restaurants.
_____ 2 There are a lot of Indian restaurants.
_____ 3 The typical restaurant has a long counter.
_____ 4 Teenagers go to burger or pizza restaurants.

Speak

4 PAIRS Do you go to restaurants or cafés? If so, how often do you go?

Listen

5 🔊 Justin is a New Yorker who is living in London. Listen to him talking about some of the differences. Take notes in the chart.

	U.S.	U.K.
Dinner times		
Portions		
Type of food		

Write

> **Writing tip: Conjunctions *both . . . and, either . . . or***
>
> We can join two things in one sentence by using pairs of conjunctions, for example, *both . . . and* or *either . . . or.*
>
> *Italian and Chinese restaurants are popular in **both** London **and** New York.*
> *People go to **either** burger **or** pizza restaurants.*

6 Write sentences in your notebook. Combine the items with *both . . . and* or *either . . . or.*

1 I like _____. (burgers + pizza).
  I like both burgers and pizza.
2 _____ (my friends + my parents) think this restaurant is too expensive.
3 She doesn't eat _____ (fish/chicken).
4 _____ (Indian + Thai) food can be very hot and spicy.
5 This restaurant doesn't accept _____ (children/dogs).
6 You can have _____ (pizza/pasta), but not both.

7 On a piece of paper, write about eating out in your town. Use *both . . . and* and *either . . . or.* Use these questions to help you.

• What type of restaurants and cafés are there?
• Where do teenagers go? • Where do you go?

> **Learning strategy: Ask for more practice**
>
> After your teacher corrects your work, look at your mistakes. If you made a lot of grammar mistakes, ask your teacher for more practice in those grammar points.

CLIL PROJECT, page 140

Which one do you like?

Grammar Indefinite pronoun *one/ones*
Vocabulary Clothes, accessories, and styles
Function Choose clothes to wear

Friends

8

Get started

1 What kinds of clothes do you like?

Presentation

2 🎧 2/31 Listen and read along. Why is Carlos wearing warm clothes?

Greg: Try this for your ski trip. This is Dad's old ski jacket.
Carlos: Mm. It's a little bright.
Greg: Why don't you try this **one** on? It's Toby's old one.
Carlos: All right. How does it look?
Greg: It looks great!! Now you need ski pants. Which **ones** do you like?
Carlos: The black **ones**. Oh. They don't look right. They're too tight.
Greg: What about these baggy **ones**?
Carlos: OK. Girls, what do you think of these pants?
Polly: They look good. But you need a flowery shirt, too!
Carlos: Very funny!
Lin: And look, pink gloves! Why don't you try them on?
Carlos: No way! I'm not wearing those! Are there any gray **ones**? They're more my style.

Phrases

🎧 2/32 Listen and repeat.

• They don't look right. • They're more my style.
• try them on

Comprehension

3 Correct the mistakes.

1 Carlos ~~doesn't need~~ ski clothes. *needs*

2 Dad's jacket is too small for Carlos.

3 The first pair of pants are too baggy.

4 Lin likes the second pair of pants.

5 Carlos likes the gloves.

Vocabulary: Clothes, accessories, and styles

4a Review. Write all the clothes you can remember in your notebook. Then check the Word bank on page 125.

b 🎧 ²/₃₃ **Extension.** Listen and repeat. Look at numbers 1–9 on the photograph on page 66 and describe the items. Use the words in the box below.

1 - *a plain pink hoodie with a zipper*

Accessories, etc.
• belt • gloves • pocket • scarf • zipper

Style
• baggy • casual • dressy • tight

Pattern

• checked   • flowery   • patterned

• plain   • polka-dotted   • striped

Grammar

Indefinite pronoun *one/ones*

Singular

Which **one** do you like?
The **one** with blue stripes.
This/That/The plain red **one**.

Plural

Which **ones** do you prefer?
The **ones** with pockets.
The baggy **ones**.

☞ Go to page 135, Master your grammar.

Practice

5 Complete the conversation with *one* or *ones*.

A: I need some gloves.
B: How about those black ¹ _____?
A: I think I prefer the bright green ² _____ .
B: What about a hat? Do you like this patterned
   ³ _____?
A: I prefer the plain ⁴ _____ .
B: OK. What about pants? I like those dark blue
   ⁵ _____ . Which ⁶ _____ do
   you like?
A: I like the ⁷ _____ with the zippers.
B: What?! I'm not going shopping with you again!

Pronunciation: /tʃ/ checked, /dʒ/ jacket

6 🎧 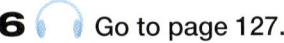 Go to page 127.

Use your English: Choose clothes to wear

7 🎧 ²/₃₆ **PAIRS** Listen and repeat. Then practice the conversation.

A: Do you like my new red shirt?
B: Yes, it looks good.
A: What should I wear with it?
B: Why don't you wear your black pants?
A: OK. Which shoes do you prefer?
B: I prefer the black ones.

Ask for advice
• What should I wear this evening?

Make suggestions
• Why don't you wear the/your . . . ?

Ask about and answer preferences
• Which one/ones do you like/prefer?
• I like/prefer the blue one/ones.

Ask for opinions
• How does/do it/they look?

Make comments
• It looks good./They look good.
• It's/They're too (baggy/tight).

---

8 **PAIRS** Practice similar conversations. Use the pictures below.

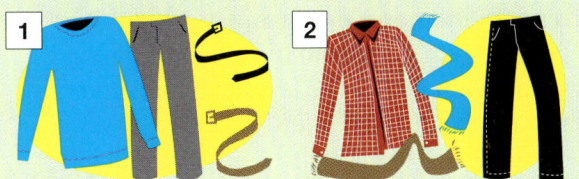

Write

9 Look at the pictures of clothes in this lesson. On a piece of paper, answer questions about them. Use *one* or *ones*.

A: *Which ski jacket do you like? Why?*
B: *I like the red one because it's bright.*

> **Extra practice**
> • **Student Book, page 120, Lesson 8A**
> • **Language Builder: WB, page 58; GB, page 124**
> • **Student CD-ROM, Unit 8**

If my friend has a problem . . .

Grammar	Conditional: *if* clause + present
Vocabulary	Personality adjectives
Function	Talk about people's personalities

Get started

1 What qualities does a "good" friend have?

Read

2 Take the quiz, then look at the key. What kind of friend are *you*?

Vocabulary: Personality adjectives

3  Listen and repeat. Then circle the words if they are positive and underline them if they are negative.

> • annoying • bad-tempered • big headed
> • bossy • cheap • easygoing • friendly
> • funny • generous • hard-working • helpful
> • honest • kind • lazy • loyal • messy • neat
> • polite • quiet • rude • shy • smart • unfriendly

File   Edit   View   Favorites   Tools   Help

What kind of friend are you?

1 If my friend has a problem, I . . .
a) listen to him or her and try to understand.
b) go out with him or her and have some fun.
c) tell him or her what to do.

2 If my friend thinks his or her homework is hard, I . . .
a) try to help him or her to understand it.
b) say, "Don't worry—it's only homework."
c) tell him or her to ask the teacher for help.

3 If my friend is sick, I usually . . .
a) visit him or her.
b) send him or her a "get well soon" text.
c) tell him or her how to get better.

4 If I don't like my friend's clothes, I . . .
a) don't tell him or her—it's not important.
b) say, "Your clothes are interesting."
c) say, "I don't like your clothes."

5 If my friend is late, I . . .
a) wait for him or her.
b) don't get angry because I'm always late.
c) text him or her and say, "Hurry up!"

6 If it's my friend's birthday, I usually . . .
a) make something for him or her.
b) choose a fun present for him or her.
c) choose a useful present for him or her.

> **KEY**
> **Mostly a)s** You are kind and helpful. You don't like telling the truth if it upsets your friends.
> **Mostly b)s** You are easygoing and fun, but you don't like listening to your friends' problems.
> **Mostly c)s** You are honest. You speak your mind, but you can sometimes be a little bossy.

4 Look at what Polly says about her friends and family. Complete each sentence with a word from the box in Exercise 3.

1 My friend Greg never says bad things about me.
He's very loyal.

2 My mother is a university teacher. She's really _____.

3 My youngest brother's bedroom is a mess. He's so _____.

4 Lin tells the truth. She's very _____.

5 My father never gets angry or shouts. He's _____.

6 My aunt is often angry. She's really _____.

7 My cousin often tells me what to do. She's kind of _____.

8 My uncle buys me a lot of presents. He's really _____.

Speak

5 **PAIRS** Complete the sentences with adjectives from Exercise 3. Then tell your partner.

1 I really like people who are _____ _easygoing_ _____.
2 I don't like people who are _____.
3 My best friend is _____.
4 I always try to be _____.
5 Sometimes I'm _____, but I try not to be.

Listen

6 Listen. Answer the questions in your notebook.

1 What does Natalie use her computer for?
2 What must you never do in a chat room?
3 What kind of person is Pablo99?
4 What kind of person is PrincessClara?
5 What happens when someone is rude?
6 What does Pablo99 say to Helen?

Grammar

> **Conditional: *if* clause + present**
>
> What **do** you **do if** your friend **has** a problem?
> **If** my friend **has** a problem, I **tell** her what to do.
> **If** I **don't like** her clothes, I **don't tell** her.

☞ Go to page 135, Master your grammar.

Practice

7 Match cues from box A to cues from box B. Write *if* clause + present sentences in your notebook.

1 – e) If an old lady needs help with a heavy bag, I always offer to carry it.

A
1 an old lady (need) help with a heavy bag
2 I (wake) up early on the weekend
3 a stranger (offer) me a ride
4 it (rain) on a Saturday
5 my mom (ask) me to clean my room
6 someone (be) rude to me
7 I (feel) a little sad
8 I really (like) a song on the radio

B
a) I always say no because it's not safe.
b) I do it immediately.
c) I usually try to go back to sleep.
d) I talk to my friends and I usually feel better.
e) I always offer to carry it.
f) I go out and buy the CD.
g) I'm still polite to him or her.
h) I stay in and surf the Internet.

Write

8 Choose three of the cues from Exercise 7, box A. Write alternative endings to make them true for you.

If I wake up early on the weekend, I get up and take a shower.

> ⊙ **Extra practice**
> • **Student Book, page 120, Lesson 8B**
> • **Language Builder: WB, page 60; GB, page 124**
> • **Student CD-ROM, Unit 8**

8c He's really cute.

Grammar	*be like* and *look like*
	Adverbs: *pretty, a little, kind of, very, really* + adjective
Vocabulary	Physical appearance
Function	Talk about people's appearance and personalities

Justin Bieber

Demi Lovato

Robert Pattinson

Taylor Swift

My favorite star

Who are your favorite stars? *TeenBeat* interviewed three teenagers about their favorites.

TB: Who's your favorite star, Rachel?

Rachel: I like Justin Bieber. He's really cute!

Luis: Justin Bieber?! He's short!

Rachel: So what? He's funny and sweet!

TB: So, Luis, you think tall people are attractive, but short people aren't?

Luis: Well, I think girls like tall guys. Robert Pattinson is 6-foot-1, and lots of girls like him!

TB: Do boys like tall girls, too?

Luis: Not really! Boys like short, pretty girls, like Demi Lovato.

Rachel: Oh, yeah? What about Taylor Swift? Do you think she's ugly?

Luis: No, she's beautiful.

Rachel: Well, she's 5-foot-11!

Luis: Are you serious?! No way!

TB: We haven't heard from you, Ella. Who's your favorite star?

Ella: Well, I like stars who look like me. I'm kind of ordinary-looking. I'm a little heavy, I wear eyeglasses, and I have braces. But there aren't very many stars who look like that!

Get started

1 Who is your favorite star? Describe him or her.

Vocabulary: Physical appearance

2a Review. In your notebook, list words you know to describe people's appearance. Then check the Word bank on page 125.

b 🎧 2/39 Extension. Listen and repeat. Then use appearance words to describe Lin, Polly, Greg, and Carlos.

General looks
- attractive • cute • handsome
- ordinary-looking • pretty
- ugly

Build
- heavy • large • medium build
- slim • thin • well-built

Read

3 🎧 2/40 Listen and read along. Who likes ordinary-looking stars? Why?

_____

_____

Comprehension

4 Read the interview and look at the photos again. Complete the chart.

	Appearance (height, build, hair, etc.)
Justin Bieber	*short,*
Robert Pattinson	
Demi Lovato	
Taylor Swift	

Grammar

be like and **look like**	
to be like (personality)	**to look like** (appearance)
What**'s** she **like**? 　She**'s** really nice. **Are** you **like** Demi? 　Yes, I **am**./No, I**'m not**.	What **does** she **look like**? 　She**'s** kind of short. 　She **has** long, dark, wavy hair. 　She **wears** eyeglasses. 　She **has** braces.
Note We often use adverbs such as *pretty*, *a little*, *kind of*, *very*, and *really* before an adjective.	

☛ Go to page 135, Master your grammar.

Practice

5 PAIRS Describe the celebrities.

Dakota Fanning

Taylor Lautner

Keke Palmer

Corbin Bleu

A: *What does Dakota Fanning look like?*
B: *She's pretty and she has long blond hair . . .*

Speak

6 PAIRS Describe your best friend, your favorite cousin, or someone else you know.

A: *Do you have a favorite cousin?*
B: *Yes, I do. His name's Cristiano.*
A: *What does he look like?*
B: *Well, he isn't handsome. He's kind of ordinary-looking.*
A: *What's he like as a person?*
B: *He's really nice, and he . . .*

Write

7 Write about your best friend on a piece of paper. Use the text below as a model.

Soledad is my best friend. She's 14 years old. She's slim and very pretty. She's tall, and she has medium-length black hair. When you first meet her, you think she's a little rude, but she's just shy.

 Extra practice
- **Student Book, page 120, Lesson 8C**
- **Language Builder: WB, page 62; GB, page 125**
- **Student CD-ROM, Unit 8**

INTEGRATED
CONSOLIDATION
SKILLS

Curriculum link: Science

Get started

1 What do you know about the celebrities in the photos?

Read

2 Read the article. Check your answers to Exercise 1. Which celebrities are friends?

Opposites attract—true or false?

Brad Pitt | George Clooney

Selena Gomez | Taylor Swift

Does your best friend have a similar personality to you, or are you and your friend very different? People often say that "opposites attract," but is it really true? Psychologists in the U.S. discovered that opposites can attract in new love relationships. If one person loves going to parties and the other person feels shy at parties, they often have a good relationship at first.

But scientists also say that these relationships don't last for a long time. For long relationships, we prefer people who are like us. Quiet people like quiet people, and good-looking people like other attractive people. Also, friends often like the same music, movies, sports, and school subjects.

Are the psychologists' ideas true? Let's look at some famous people. Brad Pitt and George Clooney became friends when they were working on the film *Ocean's Eleven*. At first they don't seem very similar. George is dark with gray hair, and Brad is blond. Brad has a big family, but George doesn't. But other things are the same. They have the same sense of humor, and they both help charities for poor people.

Selena Gomez and Taylor Swift are also good friends. Are they opposites? They look different. Selena has black hair and brown eyes, and Taylor has blond hair and blue eyes. But they are similar in other ways. Both are famous singers, both are in good shape, and both like to go out. And both dated Taylor Lautner!

> **New words and phrases**
> • opposites • attract • similar • personality • psychologists • relationship • scientist • last (*v*)
> • like (= similar to) • single • sense of humor • charity • in good shape • date (*v*)

3a Try to guess the meaning of these words from the reading on page 72.

- in good shape • relationship
- sense of humor • similar

b Use the words to complete the sentences.

1 If you and another person look and behave in the same way, you are _____ *similar* _____.

2 People who laugh at the same things have the same _____.

3 People who exercise a lot are usually _____.

4 If two people like each other and get along well, they have a good _____.

Comprehension

4 Circle the correct answer.

1 Two people who have opposite personalities
   a) like going to parties.
   b) work well together.
   c) don't often stay together for a long time.

2 People who have similar personalities
   a) usually make good friends.
   b) have different interests.
   c) are shy.

3 Brad Pitt and George Clooney
   a) look the same.
   b) like to help others.
   c) are the same age.

4 Selena Gomez and Taylor Swift
   a) don't like to sing.
   b) like staying at home.
   c) don't look similar.

5 Explain the main points from the text.

1 What interests do friends often share?

_____

2 How are the celebrity friends similar?

_____

Listen

6 2 41 Listen to Billy and Holly talking about their best friends. Complete the chart.

	Billy	Holly
Best friend	*Jake*	
Personality	*funny interesting*	
Interests		
Appearance		
Similar or opposite?		

Speak

7 PAIRS Discuss these questions.

1 Do you look similar to your best friend?
2 Do you like the same clothes?
3 Do you like doing the same things?

Write

8 On a piece of paper, write a description of you and a friend. Then say if you are similar or different.

Write about:
- your appearance
- your personalities
- your interests (sports, leisure activities)
- whether you are similar or different

I'm Esteban, and my best friend is Paul. I'm tall and dark, and he's . . .

CLIL PROJECT, page 140

Grammar (40 points)

1 Write two sentences: with *too* + adjective and *not* + adjective + *enough*. (8 points)

0 I can't read. It's ___. (noisy/quiet)

   It's too noisy.   *It's not quiet enough.*

1 These sneakers hurt. They're ___. (big/small)

   _____ _____

2 I don't like this movie. It's ___. (boring/exciting)

   _____ _____

3 My sister doesn't like computer games.
She's ___. (young/old)

   _____ _____

4 Don't move to that town. It's ___. (far/close)

   _____ _____

2 Complete the e-mail with the correct forms of the present continuous. (8 points)

```
File  Edit  View  Favorites  Tools  Help

Hi Josh,
I'm really busy tomorrow. I 0 m going_____ (go)
swimming, then my brother Mark 1_____
(play) football, so I 2_____ (watch) him.
Then we 3_____ (have) a family meal.
We 4_____ (not go) to a restaurant. Mark
and I 5_____ (cook) the meal. No, we
6_____ (not make) pizza! We
7_____ (make) roast chicken!
How about meeting up next weekend?
I 8_____ (not plan) anything special then.
Liam
```

3 Complete the conversation with the correct form of *(not) like* or *would like*. (7 points)

Dad: What 0 ___*would*___ you ___*like*___ to eat?

Liam: Chicken. I really 1_____ chicken.

Mark: Chicken's OK, but I 2_____
something different this evening.

Dad: What about pasta? You usually
3_____ pasta.

Mark: Yes, but Mom 4_____ it.

Dad: You're right. I guess she 5_____ fish.

Liam: But Mark and I 6_____ fish!

Dad: OK, what about pizza? 7_____ you
_____ a pizza this evening?

Liam: Now that's a good idea!

4 Complete with *one* or *ones*. (5 points)

Woman: Which T-shirt do you like?

Emma: (black) 0 I think I like ___*the black one*___.

Woman: OK. Which sneakers do you like?

Emma: (silver) I like 1_____.

Woman: And which shirt do you like?

Emma: (small) I like 2_____.

Woman: Now, which pants do you like?

Emma: (gray) I'm not sure. I think I like 3_____.

Woman: Which gloves do you like?

Emma: (white) The 4_____.

Woman: OK. And which hat do you like?

Emma: (red) I like 5_____.

5 Write *if* + present sentences. (12 points)

0 it/rains//he/get very wet

   If it rains, he gets very wet.

1 it/be cold//I/wear a coat

   _____

2 there/not be any snow//they/not go skiing

   _____

3 people/be rude//I/get upset

   _____

4 movies/be bad//I/leave before the end

   _____

5 there/be a lot of traffic//he/not drive to work

   _____

6 she/not like a shirt//she /not wear it

   _____

Vocabulary (40 points)

6 Write the places. (5 points)

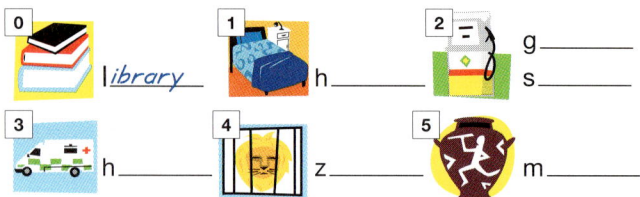

0 *library* 1 h_____ 2 g_____ s_____
3 h_____ 4 z_____ 5 m_____

7 Choose the correct word. (5 points)

0 There's nothing to do here. It's really a) noisy.
b) safe. c)(boring.)

1 The new shopping mall is always full of people. It's
very a) crowded. b) safe. c) close.

2 I can't sleep. The road outside my bedroom
window is too a) dirty. b) noisy. c) stressful.

3 It's not dangerous. It's a) cheap. b) quiet. c) safe.

4 Those shoes are great, but I can't buy them.
They're too a) relaxing. b) boring. c) expensive.

5 The air here is a) clean. b) close. c) empty.

8 Complete the crossword puzzle. Find the hidden word to finish the movie title. (6 points)

Movie title: ___, *Trains, and Automobiles*

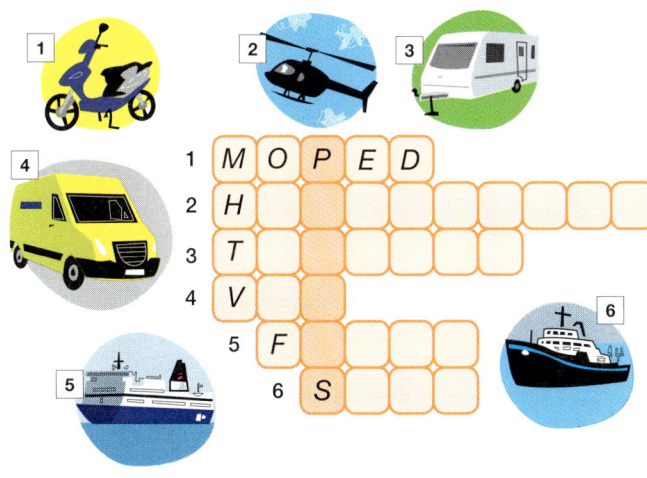

1 M O P E D
2 H
3 T
4 V
5 F
6 S

9 Complete the food phrases with words from the box. (5 points)

> • apple   • garlic   • green   • pork
> • ~~roast~~   • spaghetti

0 __*roast*__ chicken   1 _____ bread
2 _____ bolognese   3 _____ chop
4 _____ salad   5 _____ pie

10 Write the words in the chart. (19 points)

> • ~~honest~~ • ~~plain~~ • ~~slim~~ • ~~scarf~~ • generous
> • bossy • flowery • zipper • attractive
> • medium build • annoying • checked
> • glove • helpful • patterned • handsome
> • spotted • funny • belt • striped
> • well built • ugly • pretty

Pattern	Personality	Appearance	Accessory
plain	*honest*	*slim*	*scarf*

Use your English (20 points)

11 Choose the correct response. (10 points)

0 **A:** Are you ready to order?
  B: a) Yes, I'll have lasagna, please.
     b) No, thank you.   c) Me, too, please.
1 **A:** Harry's coming to visit next month.
  B: a) Come on! Who's Harry?   b) Remind me. Who's Harry?   c) It's my treat! Who's Harry?
2 **A:** Would you like fries with that?
  B: a) Can I have fries, please?
     b) Not for me, thanks.   c) Yes, I'd like.
3 **A:** Anything else?
  B: a) No way!   b) I'd like one, please.
     c) Can I have an orange juice, please?
4 **A:** Would you like a salad, too?
  B: a) No, thanks.   b) I'm ready to order.
     c) Me, too, please.
5 **A:** Do you like my new jacket?
  B: a) It's too baggy. b) I can't wait!
     c) They don't look right.

12 Complete the conversation with phrases from the box. (10 points)

> • What should I wear with it? • It's too tight.
> • How does it look? • It looks good.
> • ~~What should I wear?~~ • Which one do you prefer?

A: It's Olivia's party tomorrow. ⁰ *What should I wear?*
B: Why don't you wear your white skirt?
A: OK. Good idea. ¹_____
B: What about your green shirt?
A: I have two green shirts. ²_____
B: The flowery one, with the pockets.
A: OK. I'll put it on. ³_____
B: Wear it to the party. ⁴_____
A: How about this jacket? What do you think?
B: Don't wear that one. ⁵_____

SELF-CHECK	
Grammar	____ /40
Vocabulary	____ /40
Use your English	____ /20
Total score	____ /100

9 Out and about

Have you ever…?

Grammar	Present perfect; The definite article with places
Vocabulary	Vacation activities
Function	Talk about experiences

ALOHA! WELCOME TO HAWAII!

Are you looking for a new vacation experience?

Have you ever
- ☐ **been** to an island?
- ☐ **surfed** in the Pacific Ocean?
- ☐ **seen** a volcano?
- ☐ **been** canoeing on the sea?
- ☐ **swum** with dolphins?
- ☐ **watched** a whale swim past your boat?

You haven't? Then come to Hawaii, the U.S.'s 50th state! Try an ALOHA-VACATION!

Visitors' comments

"I**'ve never been** to Hawaii before. It's fantastic. My boyfriend's a surfer. He**'s seen** a lot of surfing beaches, but he**'s never seen** a surfing beach like Waikiki!"
—*Megan, Florida*

"We**'ve done** some canoeing in rivers, but we**'ve never done** any canoeing on the sea before. It's amazing."
—*Lucas, New York*

Get started

1 What did you do on your last vacation?

Vocabulary: Vacation activities

2 Review. List as many vacation activities as you can in your notebook. Put them in four groups. Then check the Word bank on page 125.

- in the sea: *go swimming/swim*
- on the beach • in the mountains • in town

Read

3 🎧 3/02 Listen and read along. What is the famous surfing beach in Hawaii? _____

Comprehension

4 Which of these activities are in the advertisement for Hawaii? Check (✓) the boxes.

☐ surfing ☐ mountain biking ☐ swimming
☐ whale watching ☐ sunbathing
☐ horseback riding ☐ canoeing ☐ rock climbing

Grammar

Present perfect	
Affirmative	**Negative**
I **have** / I**'ve been** to an island.	I **have not** / **haven't been** to Hawaii.
He**'s surfed** at a lot of beaches.	He **hasn't surfed** at a beach like Waikiki.
We**'ve done** some canoeing in rivers.	We **haven't done** any canoeing on the sea.
Questions	**Answers**
Have you **seen** a whale?	Yes, I **have**. / No, I **haven't**.
Has she **swum** with dolphins?	Yes, she **has**. / No, she **hasn't**.
Present Perfect with *ever* and *never*	
ever: **Questions**	*never:* **Negative**
Have you **ever been** to the Rockies?	No. I**'ve never been** to the Rockies.
Has he **ever climbed** the Himalayas?	No. He**'s never climbed** the Himalayas.

☛ Go to page 136, Master your grammar.

> **Note: The definite article with places**
> We use the definite article with the following:
> • plural countries • mountains • rivers
> • seas and oceans • groups of islands • deserts
> (**the** U.S., **the** Rockies, **the** Amazon River)

Practice

5 A Colombian friend is coming to stay with Carlos. Complete Carlos's e-mail.

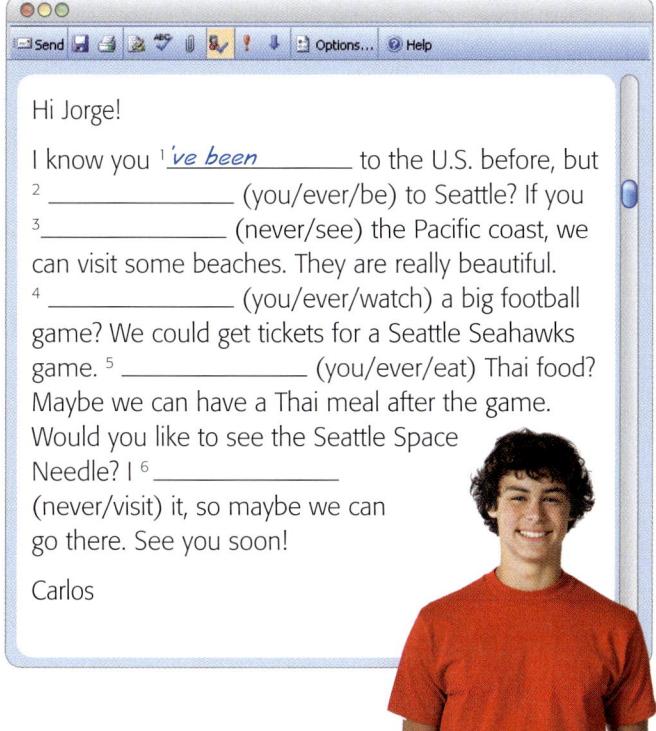

Hi Jorge!

I know you ¹ *'ve been* _____ to the U.S. before, but ² _____ (you/ever/be) to Seattle? If you ³ _____ (never/see) the Pacific coast, we can visit some beaches. They are really beautiful. ⁴ _____ (you/ever/watch) a big football game? We could get tickets for a Seattle Seahawks game. ⁵ _____ (you/ever/eat) Thai food? Maybe we can have a Thai meal after the game. Would you like to see the Seattle Space Needle? I ⁶ _____ (never/visit) it, so maybe we can go there. See you soon!

Carlos

Speak

6a **PAIRS** Ask and answer questions from the questionnaire.

A: *Have you ever been to the U.S.?*
B: *Yes, I have./No, I haven't.*

Questionnaire	
1 (go) to the U.S.?	☐
2 (see) a famous person?	☐
3 (meet) a famous person?	☐
4 (ride) a horse?	☐
5 (eat) squid?	☐
6 (swim) in the sea?	☐
7 (be) canoeing?	☐
8 (sleep) in a tent?	☐

b Tell the class about your partner.

Write

7 Write to a friend who is coming to stay. Use Carlos's e-mail in Exercise 5 to help you.

> ⊘ **Extra practice**
> • **Student Book, page 121, Lesson 9A**
> • **Language Builder: WB, page 66; GB, page 128**
> • **Student CD-ROM, Unit 9**

9B Have you put up your tent yet?

Grammar	Present perfect with *already* and *yet*
Function	Exclamations

Get started

1 Have you ever been camping? What was it like?

Presentation

2 🎧 ³⁄₀₃ Listen and read along. Why is Lin upset?

Lin: Hey, Carlos, **have** you **put up** your tent **yet**?

Carlos: Yeah, **I have**. It's that green one.

Lin: I **haven't started yet**. I borrowed this tent from Polly, but one of the poles is missing.

Carlos: Are you sure? Why don't you look in the bag?

Lin: I**'ve already looked**. It's not there. Oh, what a nightmare!

Carlos: Calm down, Lin. I found it! It was under your backpack.

Lin: That's strange! How did it get there?

Carlos: I have no idea. Come on. Let's put this tent up.

Ten minutes later:

Carlos: There you are. It's ready. It's not bad, but I think mine's nicer.

Lin: Thanks, Carlos. I owe you one . . . Oh, no! How horrible!

Carlos: What's the problem now?

Lin: I saw a spider. Oh, I hate camping!

> **Phrases**
>
> 🎧 ³⁄₀₄ Listen and repeat.
>
> - I owe you one. • Calm down,
> - What's the problem now? • I have no idea.

Comprehension

3 Complete the sentences.

1 One of Lin's tent poles _____*is missing*_____ .

2 Carlos suggests looking for the pole in

_____ .

3 The pole was _____ .

4 Carlos thinks that his tent is _____ .

5 When the tent is ready, Lin sees _____ .

Grammar

Present perfect with *already* and *yet*
Affirmative
She**'s already looked**.
Negative
I **haven't started yet**.
Questions
Have you **put up** your tent **yet**? **Have** you **already looked**?
Short answers
Yes, I **have**./No, I **haven't**.

☛ Go to page 136, Master your grammar.

Use your English: Exclamations

6 🎧 3/07 **PAIRS Listen and repeat. Then practice the conversation.**

A: Have you opened your birthday presents yet?
B: Yes, I have. My uncle gave me a new laptop!
A: What a fantastic present!
B: Unfortunately, I've already broken it!
A: What a nightmare!

Exclamations:

Surprise
- What a surprise! • Wow! • How strange/weird!
- No way! • You're kidding! • That's incredible!

Pleasure
- That's good/great! • How amazing/nice!
- What a fantastic present/show/evening!

Horror
- What a nightmare! • That's awful!
- How horrible/disgusting!

Disappointment
- What a pity! • That's a shame!

---

7 **PAIRS Practice similar conversations with the cues below. Use *Luckily* or *Unfortunately*.**

1 you/eat? (Yes/I/eat/three burgers) (I/be/still hungry)
A: *Have you eaten yet?*
B: *Yes, I have. I ate three burgers! . . .*

2 you/buy a new cell phone? (Yes/I/buy/a cool phone) (I/lose it)

3 you/go camping? (Yes/we/go to the beach) (It/be warm and sunny)

Practice

4 Complete the conversation using the cues and *yet* or *already*.

Mr. West: Good morning, Lin. Your hair's wet!
¹ *Have you already taken a shower* (you/take a shower)?
Lin: Yes, I have.
Mr. West: ² _____ (you/have breakfast), too?
Lin: Yes, I have.
Mr. West: Good. ³ _____ (Carlos/have breakfast)?
Lin: No, he hasn't. ⁴ _____ (He/not get up). . . . Oh, there he is.
Mr. West: Hurry up, Carlos. ⁵ _____ (The other students/have breakfast).
Carlos: Sorry, Mr. West. I didn't sleep well. I had a bad dream about spiders!

Pronunciation: /ʊ/ p<u>u</u>t, /u/ d<u>o</u>

5 🎧 Go to page 127.

Write

8 Imagine you are on a camping trip. On a piece of paper, write a diary entry about it. Use the present perfect with *already* and *yet*.

May 20: We've already been here two days. I've seen lots of wild animals and . . .

> **Extra practice**
> - **Student Book, page 121, Lesson 9B**
> - **Language Builder: WB, page 68; GB, page 129**
> - **Student CD-ROM, Unit 9**

He gave rock lessons.

Grammar	Simple past and present perfect
Vocabulary	Types of music
Function	Talk about music events and activities

Get started

1 Who's your favorite singer or band . . .

a) when you want to relax? b) when you're happy?
c) when you're traveling?

Vocabulary: Types of music

2a Review. Write a list of types of music in your notebook. Then check the Word bank on page 125.

b What type of music do or did the people below write or play? Label the photos.

1 **Bob Marley**
  reggae

3 **Beethoven**
  _____

2 **Iron Maiden**
  _____

4 **Jay-Z**
  _____

Read

3 🎧 ³⁄₀₈ Listen and read along. How many schools of rock are there in the U.S.? _____

School of ROCK

Have you seen the movie *School of Rock*? It's about a rock musician who became a teacher. The movie is based on a real music school that is run by Paul Green. Paul Green started the first School of Rock in 1998 in Philadelphia in the U.S. He gave students rock music lessons after school, but he wanted to do more. Now he gives them the chance to play in rock concerts. "Some of our students have never played in front of a real audience before. We teach them how to do it," he says. He has already taught hundreds of young people to be rock music performers, and now there are over 30 schools of rock in different towns in the U.S.

5 **Louis Armstrong**
  _____

6 **Miley Cyrus**
  _____

Comprehension

4 Read the article and answer the questions.

1 What is the movie *School of Rock* about?

2 When did Paul Green start his first rock school?

3 What does he teach his students to do?

4 How many students has he taught?

Grammar

> ### Simple past and present perfect
>
> **Simple past**
>
> He **started** the school in **1998**.
>
> **Present perfect**
>
> He **has** already **taught** hundreds of young people to be rock musicians.

☞ Go to page 136, Master your grammar.

Practice

5 Complete the conversation with the simple past or present perfect.

Greg: Hi, Carlos. What ¹ *did you do* (do) last night?

Carlos: I ² _____ (go) to a fantastic concert.

Greg: Who ³ _____ (see)?

Carlos: I ⁴ _____ (see) the Jets.

Greg: Who? I ⁵ _____ (never/hear) of them. What type of music do they play?

Carlos: Mostly rock, but they ⁶ _____ (play) some great Latin music last night.

Greg: Cool. Hey, ⁷ _____ (you/ever/be) to a Corbin Bleu concert? He's playing here this weekend. Do you want to go?

Carlos: Sure! I ⁸ _____ (never/see) him in concert before!

6 In your notebook, write two sentences using the simple past and the present perfect.

1 I/have/lunch.   a) an hour ago   b) already

   a) I had lunch an hour ago.

   b) I've already had lunch.

2 Polly/buy/a guitar?   a) already   b) yesterday

3 My parents/visit the U.S.   a) never   b) in 2008

4 My brother/see/*Avatar*   a) not yet   b) last night

Listen

7 🔊 3/09 Listen to an interview with Charlie, a teenage musician. Correct the sentences.

          Seattle

1 Charlie is from ~~New York~~.

2 He started playing the guitar when he was five.

3 He writes rap songs.

4 He doesn't like playing rock music.

5 He has played concerts in stadiums.

6 He hasn't made a CD yet.

Speak

8 PAIRS Ask and answer the questions.

1 be/to a concert? (When/go? Who/see?)

   A: *Have you ever been to a rock concert?*

   B: *Yes, I have . . .*

2 have/music lessons? (When?) (What instrument/play?)

3 see/a famous singer? (Who? When?)

Write

9 In your notebook, write a paragraph about your favorite singer or band. Use the simple past and the present perfect.

My favorite singer is Beyoncé. She was in the band Destiny's Child before, but now she sings alone. She has already won 16 Grammy awards! . . .

> **Extra practice**
> - **Student Book, page 121, Lesson 9C**
> - **Language Builder: WB, page 70; GB, page 129**
> - **Student CD-ROM, Unit 9**

INTEGRATED
CONSOLIDATION
SKILLS

Values for living

Get started

1 What are the qualities of a good leader?

A good leader is popular ...

Read

2 Read the story. Who wins the first challenge? _____

> **New words and phrases**
> - challenge • leader • course • rule
> - as a team • intelligence • compass
> - find your way back • Good luck!
> - keep (kept) • lost • read the map • hurt
> - against the rules • Congratulations!

The challenge

Jack arrived at the Seattle Outdoor Challenge Center and went to the hall where Mr. Riley, the leader of the center, was speaking.

"This is a two-day course about being a leader," Mr. Riley said. "There are two challenges. Try to finish them, but remember the rules. One: Work as a team. Two: Don't do anything dangerous. And three: Use your intelligence."

For the first challenge, Mr. Riley took groups to a forest, about 3 miles from the center.

"It's 3:30. I've given you a map and a compass. You must find your way back to the center. The first team back is the winner. Good luck!"

Jack was on a team with Lisa, Ed, and Kim. "Hi," Jack said. "We haven't met before, but I'm usually the leader at school. Can I be the leader of our group?"

"Why don't we just work as a team?" Lisa asked.

"It's better if I'm the leader," Jack said. He kept the map and the compass.

Half an hour later, Jack and his team were lost.

"Why don't I read the map?" Lisa said.

"Good idea," Ed said. "I hurt my ankle, so let's get back quickly."

"I have a better idea," Jack replied. "There's a house over there. I'm going to ask for a ride."

"Are you crazy?" Lisa said. "It's against the rules."

"Which rules?" Jack asked. "Ed has hurt his ankle, and Mr. Riley said, 'Use your intelligence.' Come on, let's go."

Twenty minutes later, Jack, Lisa, Kim, and Ed arrived back at the center in a car. They walked into the center, where Mr. Riley was working on his computer.

"Congratulations!" said Mr. Riley. "You are the winners. How do you feel?"

Lisa, Ed, and Kim looked at Jack. "Why don't you ask our leader?" said Lisa.

Comprehension

3 Answer the questions.

1 What is Jack's course about?
being a leader

2 What is the first challenge?
_____

3 How many people are on Jack's team?
_____

4 Who is reading the map?
_____

5 Where is the team after 30 minutes?
_____

6 Why did Jack's team win the challenge?
_____

 Solve it!

4 How long did it take Jack and the team to complete the challenge?

Speak your mind!

> **Speaking tip: Use gestures or mime when speaking**
> Use gestures or mime if you can't think of a word you need. Don't stop speaking.

5a What is the difference between a good leader and a bad leader? Write *G* (*good*) or *B* (*bad*) for each phrase.

- is confident — G
- listens to other people — ☐
- makes all the decisions — ☐
- always wants to win — ☐
- is positive — ☐
- never says, "I don't know" — ☐
- gets angry — ☐
- breaks the rules — ☐

b PAIRS Discuss the questions.

1 Was Jack a good leader? Why or Why not?
2 Were Jack, Lisa, Ed, and Kim a good team?
3 Do you think Jack was wrong when he asked for a ride?

Listen

> **Learning strategy: Pay attention to key words**
> When you listen or read, pay attention to key words. They often contain important information, and they are usually stressed.

6 🎧 3/10 Mr. Riley talks to the kids after the challenge. Listen and answer the questions.

1 Why did Jack enjoy the challenge?
He enjoyed it because he won.

2 Why didn't Lisa enjoy the challenge?
_____

3 What is Mr. Riley's first rule for leaders?
_____

4 What is his second rule for leaders?
_____

5 Why is he angry that they asked for a ride?
_____

6 What does he say about winning?
_____

Write

7 Imagine you are Lisa. On a piece of paper, complete the letter to a friend telling him about the course.

> Dear Patrick,
>
> How are you? I'm writing this letter from the SOC Center in Seattle. I'm taking a course here. It's . . .
>
> We had a difficult challenge today. Mr. Riley took us to . . .
>
> I was in a group with . . . and the leader of our team was . . .
>
> After only half an hour . . .
>
> Jack wanted to . . .
>
> Twenty minutes later . . .

CLIL PROJECT, page 140

83

Technology

It will fly at 3,000 mph.

Grammar	*will* for predictions
Function	Talk about the future

Get started

1 Have you ever traveled by plane? Would you like to travel on the plane in the photo below? Why or why not?

Read

2  Listen and read along. What's the name of the plane in the photo? _____

Comprehension

3 Read the article. Match facts a)–f) to topics 1–6.

_c_	1	name of plane	a) over 100,000 ft
____	2	time for trip	b) 3,000 mph
____	3	speed of plane	c) the *A2*
____	4	altitude of flight	d) $3,000
____	5	number of passengers	e) about 5 hours
____	6	price of a ticket	f) 300

💡 Solve it!

4 Read the text. How far is it from London to Sydney in Australia? _____

10

Future Flight!

This is a computer drawing of the plane of the future. British engineers and scientists have published plans for a new hypersonic plane called the *A2*. It **will be** very fast. At the moment, a flight from London in the U.K. to Sydney in Australia takes about 21 hours, but with the *A2*, the same flight **will take** under 5 hours.

The plane **will fly** at 3,000 miles per hour and will fly at an altitude of over 100,000 feet.

It **will carry** 300 passengers, but it **won't have** any windows because scientists haven't found glass that is strong enough. It **will be** better for the environment than other planes because the engines **won't produce** gases that cause pollution.

In the future, **will** people **travel** to Australia for the weekend? It's possible! But how much **will** a ticket **cost**? The planners say that it **won't be** very expensive—about $3,000. The *A2* **will be** ready for its first flight in 2020.

Grammar

will for predictions

Affirmative	Negative
The plane **will fly** at 3,000 mph.	It **won't (will not) have** windows.
Questions	**Short answers**
Will people **buy** tickets?	Yes, they **will.** / No, they **won't.**

☛ Go to page 137, Master your grammar.

Practice

5 *Rocketship Three* is a new spaceplane that will carry tourists into space. Look at the factfile below. Complete the questions and answers.

1 When __*will*__ the first flight be?   __*In 2015*__.
2 How many people _____ it carry?   _____.
3 How long _____ the trip take?   _____.
4 How high _____ the spaceplane fly?   _____.
5 How fast _____ the spaceplane fly?   _____.
6 How much _____ a ticket cost?   _____.
7 _____ people have a meal?   _____.
8 _____ the spaceplane have windows? _____.

See Earth from space!

1 First flight: 2015   **5** Speed: 2,000 mph
2 Passengers: 6   **6** Ticket: $230,000
3 Trip time: 2.5 hours   **7** A meal: ✗
4 Altitude: 68 miles   **8** Windows: ✓

Rocketship Three

6 Complete the *Tomorrow's World* website with *'ll, will,* or *won't* and the verbs in parentheses.

File   Edit   View   Favorites   Tools   Help

"I'm sure robots [1] __*will cook*__ (cook) and clean for us. We [2] _____ (not/do) any housework."—**IAN**

"Machines [3] _____ (do) everything. Then what [4] _____ we _____ (do)? I think we [5] _____ (get) bored!"—**JAN**

"I think people [6] _____ (have) vacations on the moon, but many people [7] _____ (not/go). It [8] _____ (be) too expensive."—**LI**

"Everyone [9] _____ (ride) bikes. People [10] _____ (not/drive)."—**KIM**

Pronunciation: /aʊ/ n**ow**, /oʊ/ kn**ow**

7 🎧 Go to page 127.

Speak

8 **PAIRS** Ask about and answer the ideas in Exercise 6.

A: *Will robots cook and clean for us?*
B: *Yes, I think they will.*

Listen

9 🎧 ³/₁₄ Listen. What does Matt talk about? Complete the chart with checks (✓) or Xs.

1 computers	✓	5 trees	
2 cell phones		6 sports	
3 homework		7 teachers	
4 books		8 home study	

Write

10 On a piece of paper, write predictions about schools in the future. Use ideas from Exercise 9.

Schools will use more computers in the future . . .

> **Extra practice**
> • **Student Book, page 121, Lesson 10A**
> • **Language Builder: WB, page 74; GB, page 132**
> • **Student CD-ROM, Unit 10**

Grammar	Conditional: *if* clause + future
Vocabulary	Computer language
Function	Talk about real possibilities

Get started

1 Do you know how to use a computer? What can you do?

Presentation

2 🎧 3/15 Listen and read along. Who's the e-mail from?

Carlos: How's the computer class going, Grandma?

Grandma: Well, I can send and receive e-mails now!

Carlos: Great. Can you surf the net, too?

Grandma: Of course. I've even downloaded music.

Carlos: Cool. **If I have** time tomorrow, **I'll burn** a CD for you.

Grandma: OK, thank you. Now, **what will happen if I open** this? It's an e-mail attachment called "I love you!"

Carlos: No, wait! It's probably a virus. The computer **will crash if** you **open** it.

Grandma: Oh, dear. Too late.

Carlos: It's OK. It's an e-card from Dad.

Comprehension

3 Write *Carlos* or *Grandma*.

1 ___*Grandma*___ is learning to use computers.
2 _____ got some new music.
3 _____ offers to make a CD.
4 _____ says there is a virus.
5 _____ opens an attachment.

Vocabulary: Computer language

4a 🎧 3/16 Listen and repeat. Check the Word bank on page 125.

b Match the photos to the words in the box. Write the numbers of the photos.

> __ attachment __ e-mail __ keyboard
> __ laptop __ mouse __ memory stick
> __ PC (desktop computer) __ printer
> __ scanner _1_ screen __ software

c Which objects can you find in the photo above? _____
_____

5 Complete the text with nouns and verbs from the boxes on pages 86 and 125.

Computer skills for students

E-mails

You must know how to ¹ ___send___ and ² _____ e-mails. You must also know how to ³ _____ a file to an e-mail. But be careful when you ⁴ _____ an attachment! It might have a ⁵ _____ .

The Internet

You must know how to ⁶ _____ to the net and ⁷ _____ for information. You must also know how to ⁸ _____ pictures and music from the net.

Grammar

Conditional: *if* clause + future

Statements

If I **have** time, **I'll** burn a CD.
If I **buy** that software, I **won't have** problems.
The computer **will crash if** you **open** that.

Questions

What **will happen if** I **open** this?
If I **have** a problem, **will** you **help** me?

Short answers

Yes, I **will.**/No, I **won't.**

☛ Go to page 137, Master your grammar.

<section>

Practice

6 Some students are in the computer room. Write *if* clause + future sentences in your notebook.

If the computer crashes, I'll lose my files.

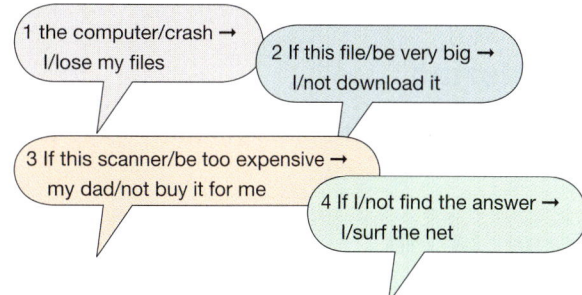

1 the computer/crash → I/lose my files
2 If this file/be very big → I/not download it
3 If this scanner/be too expensive → my dad/not buy it for me
4 If I/not find the answer → I/surf the net

7 Match cues from box A to cues from box B. Write *if* clause + future sentences in your notebook.

1- b) If the bus is late, we'll miss the start of the movie.

A
1 If the bus/be late
2 you/help me
3 If she/not call you
4 you/not get a virus
5 your mom/be angry

B
a) you/call her?
b) we/miss the start of the movie
c) if we/get home late?
d) if I/have problems with my homework?
e) if you/not open e-mails from strangers

Speak

8 **PAIRS** What will you do this Saturday? Use the cues to answer the question.

If it's sunny on Saturday, I'll go for a bike ride.

• it's sunny • I don't have any homework
• my friends don't call me • I'm tired

Write

9 Write *if* clause + future sentences in your notebook about your Saturday plans.

> **Extra practice**
> • **Student Book, page 122, Lesson 10B**
> • **Language Builder: WB, page 76; GB, page 133**
> • **Student CD-ROM, Unit 10**

<section>

10c I'll be more careful.

Grammar	*will* for decisions/promises
	will for offers
Vocabulary	Problems
Function	Describe and deal with problems

Get started

1 Have you ever had a problem with a computer? What went wrong?

Presentation

2 Listen and read along. What's wrong with Carlos's laptop?

Man: Hello. Can I help you?

Carlos: Yes, I have a problem with my laptop.

Man: What's the matter with it?

Carlos: The keyboard doesn't work, and the screen's cracked, too.

Man: How did that happen?

Carlos: I was carrying it to school and I dropped it.

Man: OK, **I'll look** at it for you. **I'll** probably **need** to send it away.

Carlos: OK. How long **will** it **take**?

Man: Two weeks. **I'll call** you when it's ready.

Carlos: OK. **I'll** be more careful with it from now on!

Comprehension

3 Correct the mistakes.

laptop

1 Carlos has a problem with his ~~piano~~

2 Carlos left his laptop at school.

3 The man will e-mail when the laptop is ready.

4 The laptop will be ready in two days.

💡 Solve it!

4 It's September 14. On which date can Carlos pick up his laptop?

Grammar

will for decisions/promises
I'll be more careful with it from now on.
I **won't drop** it on the sidewalk again.
will for offers
I'll look at it for you.

☛ Go to page 137, Master your grammar.

Practice

5 You are with your grandparents. In your notebook, write offers to help them, using the verbs in the box.

> • do • look at • make • record • wash

1 There are a lot of dishes to do after dinner.
  I'll do the dishes.

2 Your grandmother would like a cup of coffee.
3 Their car is dirty.
4 There's a problem with their washing machine.
5 They need to record a show on TV.

Vocabulary: Problems

6 🎧 3/18 Listen and repeat. Then match the adjectives (a–h) to the objects (1–8) and make sentences.

> a) stained b) scratched c) dead d) dirty
> e) broken f) cracked g) torn h) missing

| 1 | jeans/ *g) torn* |
The jeans are torn.

| 2 | cup/_____ |

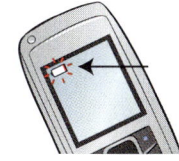

| 3 | glass/_____ |

| 4 | battery/_____ |

| 5 | button/_____ |

| 6 | jacket/_____ |

| 7 | table/_____ |

| 8 | car/_____ |

Use your English: Describe and deal with problems

7 🎧 3/19 **PAIRS** Listen and repeat. Then practice the conversation.

A Dad, I have a problem with my cell phone.
B: What's the matter with it?
A: The battery's dead.
B: I'll charge it for you.
A: That would be great. Thanks.

> **State a problem**
> • I have a problem with my laptop.
> • There's something wrong with my laptop.
>
> **Ask about a problem**
> • What's the problem? • What's the matter with it?
> • What's wrong with it?
>
> **Describe a problem**
> • It doesn't work.   • The battery's dead.
> • It's cracked/scratched/dirty/broken.
>
> **Offer to help**
> • I'll ask them to repair/clean it for you.
>
> **Say thank you**
> • Yes, please. That would be great.
> • Thanks. That's really kind of you.

8 **PAIRS** Practice similar conversations. Use the cues.

Your item	The problem	Friend's offer
jacket	a button's missing	look for a button
watch	it's broken	fix it
laptop	it's dirty	clean it

Write

9 On a piece of paper, write a paragraph about a problem you have and how to solve it.

My shirt is torn. I'll ask my mom to fix it for me …

> 🔸 **Extra practice**
> • **Student Book, page 122, Lesson 10C**
> • **Language Builder: WB, page 78; GB, page 133**
> • **Student CD-ROM, Unit 10**

INTEGRATED CONSOLIDATION SKILLS

Across cultures

Linking the world

Because of the Internet, people from all over the world can now be friends even if they never meet! Michelle and Kenji are online friends. They tell us how they use their computers.

Michelle, 16, New York, U.S.

"When I'm doing a school project, I use my computer to go online and search the Internet for information. Then I write the project on the computer. Right now I'm doing one on the Brazilian rain forest. If I find some good photos, I'll include them. And, of course, I use my computer to stay in touch with friends like Kenji. We usually chat online once or twice a week."

Kenji, 15, Manchester, U.K.

"I'm on my computer from 8 until 10 o'clock every evening. I use it to chat with Michelle, play games, check the latest soccer news, and chat about my favorite team, Manchester City. If they win the match this Saturday, I'll be really happy. Unfortunately, Michelle isn't interested in sports!"

Get started

1 Do you have a computer at home? How often do you use it?

Read

2a Read the website article. How many hours does Kenji spend on his computer every day? _____

b Read the computer factfile. How many teenagers can connect to the Internet in the U.S. and U.K.? _____

Computer factfile

 Almost all American and British teenagers (96%) have a personal computer. What do they use their computers for?

97% – to connect to the Internet (e.g., for help with school work and to buy things)
74% – for instant messaging
68% – to listen to music
63% – to play games
60% – to send e-mails
21% – to talk in chat rooms

 How often do American and British teenagers go online?

81% spend 5–10 hours per week online
50% go online every day

Comprehension

3a Read the article again. Complete the sentences.

1 Michelle and Kenji are _____*friends*_____.

2 They _____ once or twice a week.

3 Michelle talks to Kenji _____.

4 When she does school projects, Michelle usually finds _____ on the Internet.

5 Kenji goes online _____.

6 Kenji loves _____.

b Read the computer factfile again and number the activities in order of popularity: *1* = most important, *6* = least important.

- [ ] listening to music
- [ ] playing games
- [ ] sending e-mails
- [ ] chatting with friends
- [1] surfing the net
- [ ] instant messaging

c How many hours a week do most teenagers spend online? _____

Listen

4 🔊 3/20 A reporter for a computer magazine is doing a survey. Listen and complete the chart.

	Adam	Miguel
How many computers are there in the family?	2	
How often does he use it?		
What does he use it for?		
What did he last use it for?		
How can he get a new computer?		

Speak

5 GROUPS Do a computer survey. In your notebook, write two more questions. Then ask all the questions. Take notes on how many students do each activity.

1 Do you go online every day?
2 Do you use a computer to search for information?
3 Do you have online friends?

Write

Writing tip: Quantifiers *all, most, some, a few*

We use quantifiers such as *all*, *most*, *some*, and *a few* to talk in general terms about numbers of people or things.

Almost all **teenagers** have a computer.

Most teenagers use the computer to send e-mails.

Some teenagers use instant messaging.

A few teenagers use their computers to shop online.

6 In your notebook, write statements about Kenji's school in the U.K. Start your sentences with *all*, *most*, *some*, or *a few*.

1 *All students start school at 8:40 A.M.*

1 start school at 8:40 A.M.	100%
2 learn two foreign languages	40%
3 have computer classes	70%
4 have private lessons at school	10%

Learning strategy: Use graphic organizers

Use graphic organizers such as charts and diagrams to organize your notes and present information clearly.

7 On a piece of paper, write a chart about how people in your group or class use computers. Use your survey results from Exercise 5, and use the charts in this lesson as models. Then write a paragraph describing the results. Include *all*, *most*, *some*, and *a few*.

In my group, almost all students go online . . .

CLIL PROJECT, page 140

Grammar (40 points)

1 Complete with the present perfect. (7 points)

0 _Have you ever been_ (you/ever/be) skiing?

1 _____ (I/never/try) snowboarding.

2 _____ (he/ever/sleep) in a tent?

3 _____ (they/ever/meet) a big star?

4 _____ (we/watch) lots of movies this year.

5 _____ (you/ever/do) anything scary?

6 _____ (she/play) the guitar on stage.

7 _____ (I/never/learn) to play the piano.

2 Complete in the present perfect. Use verbs from the box and *already* or *yet*. (6 points)

> • buy • not speak • get up • win • ~~not see~~
> • leave • start

0 _I haven't seen The Karate Kid yet._

1 I _____ a CD player. It was $50.

2 The concert _____. It started an hour ago.

3 The new girl's name is Ann. I _____ to her _____.

4 We _____ ten matches this year.

5 Joe _____ for school. He left an hour ago.

6 It's 9 o'clock. _____ Keira _____?

3 Complete Neil's letter with the verbs in the present perfect or simple past. (10 points)

Dear Aunt Emma,

Thank you for the money. It ⁰___ _arrived_ ___ (arrive) last week, and I ¹_____ (already/spend) it! I ²_____ (go) shopping, and I ³_____ (buy) a laptop. I ⁴_____ (never/have) a laptop before. I ⁵_____ (already/download) some songs onto it. Mom ⁶_____ (come) back from Paris. She ⁷_____ (have) a great time, and the weather ⁸_____ (be) great. ⁹_____ (be) your vacation nice? We ¹⁰_____ (not have) our vacation yet.

Lots of love, Neil

4 Complete with *will* and the correct form of the verbs. (12 points)

0 If the library ___ _is_ ___ shut, I _'ll read_ at home. (read)

1 I _____ her flowers if they _____ expensive. (buy/not be)

2 If we _____ now, we _____ late. (leave/not be)

3 _____ you _____ me that photo if I _____ you my e-mail address? (send/give)

4 They _____ us if we _____ quietly. (not hear/speak)

5 If Dad _____ home soon, we _____ him to drive us to the concert. (get/ask)

6 If she _____, she _____ the test. (not study/not pass)

5 Complete with *'ll* or *won't*. (5 points)

0 **A:** Do you like the red one?
  B: No, I don't. I think I _'ll_ buy the blue one.

1 **A:** My bag is in the car.
  B: I _____ get it for you.

2 **A:** Have you gotten her a present yet?
  B: No. I _____ get her one tomorrow.

3 **A:** You're late for class!
  B: Sorry. It _____ happen again.

4 **A:** Can you help me with the party?
  B: OK. I _____ come to your house early.

5 **A:** The concert starts at 7 o'clock.
  B: Don't worry! We _____ be late.

Vocabulary (40 points)

6 Match the activities with the people. (8 points)

> a) canoeing b) climbing c) horseback riding
> d) mountain biking e) shopping f) skiing
> g) swimming h) surfing i) whale watching

_h_ 0 Leah fell and got wet on Waikiki beach.

___ 1 Jake fell in the snow.

___ 2 Luz went up a tall mountain.

___ 3 Hu saw a very big animal in the sea.

___ 4 Victor bought a coat.

___ 5 Yuri was in a boat on a lake.

___ 6 Macy rode an animal.

___ 7 Gerry spent time in a pool.

___ 8 Stan fell off his bike.

7 Unscramble the music words. (8 points)

0 iph-ohp ___hip-hop___ 1 natli _____

2 thonec _____ 3 eeggar _____

4 lofk _____ 5 islslcaca _____

6 ahvye lamet _____ 7 uosl _____

8 nutocry dna stenwre _____

8 Match the numbers to the words. (7 points)

> _____ screen ___0___ keyboard _____ scanner
>
> _____ desktop computer _____ memory stick
>
> _____ printer _____ software _____ mouse

9 Complete with computer words. (10 points)

1 How often do you [0] receive _____ and [1] s_____d
e-mails?

2 [2] S_____e your essay so you don't lose it. You
can [3] d_____e it if you don't want it later on.

3 I'll [4] d_____d the songs to my laptop.

4 Why don't you [5] a_____h the file to an e-mail?

5 If I need to [6] s_____h for information,
I usually [7] s_____f the Internet first.

6 Oh, no! I don't want my computer to [8] c_____h!

7 I need to [9] c_____t to the Internet.

8 I like this text. Can you [10] p_____t it for me?

10 Complete the problems. (7 points)

0 The carpet is a) cracked. b) stained. c) broken.

1 My cell phone battery is a) torn. b) scratched.
c) dead.

2 The cup didn't break, but it was a) stained.
b) cracked. c) missing.

3 The table is a) scratched. b) torn. c) dead.

4 I can't find my bike. It's a) dirty. b) cracked.
c) missing.

5 My jacket is a) torn. b) scratched. c) cracked.

6 The TV is a) dead. b) broken. c) stained.

7 My jeans are a) scratched. b) dirty. c) broken.

Use your English (20 points)

11 Choose the correct response. (10 points)

0 A: Here's your wallet. You left it in our car.
B: a) Thanks. I owe you one. b) Thanks. I have
no idea.   c) Thanks. How horrible!

1 A: Oh, no! I lost my bag!
B: a) How nice! b) What a pity! It's here.
c) Calm down. It's here.

2 A: Look! There's a cat hair in my sandwich!
B: a) How disgusting! b) I'll look at it for you.
c) That's great!

3 A: Have you seen this website? It's great.
B: a) Wow! b) Yes, please.
c) What's the matter with it?

4 A: I saw Selena Gomez after the concert, and she
signed my T-shirt!
B: a) That's a shame.   b) What's the problem now?
c) No way!

5 A: Oh, no! What a nightmare!
B: a) What's the problem?   b) How amazing!
c) I owe you one.

12 Look at the scrambled conversations below.
Number the lines in the correct order. (10 points)

Conversation 1

___ a) What's the problem?

___ b) OK. I'll call you when it's ready.

___ c) The screen's broken.

___ d) Yes, please. That would be great.

_1_ e) I have a problem with my phone.

___ f) Should I ask them to repair it?

Conversation 2

___ a) It hurts when I play football.

___ b) Thanks. It hurts here, near the ankle.

___ c) What's the matter with it?

___ d) Hmm. It doesn't look very good. I think you
should see the doctor.

_1_ e) There's something wrong with my foot.

___ f) OK, take your shoe off and I'll look at it.

SELF-CHECK	
Grammar	_____ /40
Vocabulary	_____ /40
Use your English	_____ /20
Total score	_____ /100

We should go home.

Grammar	*should/shouldn't*
Vocabulary	Illness
Function	Say what the matter is and give advice

Dilemmas

11

Get started

1 Look at the photo. Who feels sick?

Presentation

2 Listen and read along. What are the friends planning to do?

Carlos: This is great. I can't wait to go on the underground tour.

Polly: I think we **should join** the line. The last tour starts in ten minutes.

Greg: What's the matter, Lin? Are you OK?

Lin: No, I don't feel very well. I have a headache, and I feel really hot. Maybe I **shouldn't come** on the tour.

Greg: Hey, guys. Lin doesn't feel very well. I hate to say this, but I think we **should go** home with her.

Carlos: But these tickets cost a ton! We can't go home!

Greg: Yes, we can. With a little luck, we can get our money back.

Phrases

 Listen and repeat.

- cost a ton! • With a little luck,
- I hate to say this • I can't wait

Comprehension

3 Answer the questions.

1 Why is Carlos excited?
2 Why should they join the line?
3 Why does Greg want to leave?
4 Were the tickets expensive?

💡 Solve it!

4 Look at the sign below. What time is it in the conversation?

Seattle Underground Tour
Every hour
11.00 A.M.–5:00 P.M.

Vocabulary: Illness

5 🔊 3/23 Listen and repeat. Label the pictures with the words in the box.

> I have . . .
> • a cold • a cough • a headache
> • a sore throat • ~~a temperature~~ • an earache
> • a stomachache • a toothache • the flu
> • a pain in my (wrist)
>
> • I don't feel very well. • I feel ill/sick/hot.
> • My (wrist) hurts.

  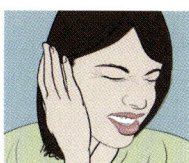

1 _a temperature_ **2** _____ **3** _____

  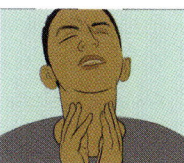

4 _____ **5** _____ **6** _____

Grammar

should/shouldn't	
Affirmative	**Negative**
We **should go** home.	We **shouldn't stay**.
Questions	**Short answers**
What **should** we **do**?	We **should** go.
Should we **go** with her?	Yes, we **should**./
	No, we **shouldn't**.

☞ Go to page 138, Master your grammar.

Practice

6 Write conversations in your notebook. Use _should_ or _shouldn't_ and the cues.

1 a cold ➜ go to bed/go out
  A: _I have a cold._
  B: _You should go to bed. You shouldn't go out._
2 a sore throat ➜ swim/drink orange juice
3 toothache ➜ eat candy/go to the dentist
4 sick ➜ go to bed/go to school
5 headache ➜ take a painkiller/listen to loud music

Use your English: Say what the matter is and give advice

7 🔊 3/24 **PAIRS** Listen and repeat. Then practice the conversation.

A: You don't look very well. Are you OK?
B: Not really. I have a temperature.
A: That's too bad. You should go home.
B: I can't. I'm too busy.

> **Ask what the matter is**
> • You don't look very well. Are you OK?
> • What's the matter?
>
> **Say what the matter is**
> • I have a (bad) cold.   • I feel sick.
>
> **Sympathize**
> • That's too bad.
>
> **Give advice**
> • You should . . .
>   – go to bed/the doctor/the dentist
>   – take some medicine/a painkiller
>
> **Accept or reject advice**
> • Yes, you're right./That's a good idea.
> • No, I don't like going to the doctor.
> • I can't. I'm too busy.

8 **PAIRS** Practice similar conversations. Use the illnesses in Exercise 5.

Write

9 Read the conversation between Lin and her friends on page 94. On a piece of paper, write a paragraph about how to solve their problems.
Lin feels sick. She shouldn't go on the tour. She should . . .

> **Extra practice**
> • **Student Book, page 122, Lesson 11A**
> • **Language Builder: WB, page 82; GB, page 136**
> • **Student CD-ROM, Unit 11**

11B She has to help her mother.

Get started

1 What are *household chores*? Should teens do them? Why or why not?

Read

2 [3 25] Listen and read along. What does Rebeka do? _____

A Teenager Who Cares

Some teenagers have one disabled parent. But Rebeka Willett, a teenager in Modesto, California, has two. Her mother, Tammy, has cerebral palsy. She can't walk or talk. To get around, she *has to use* a wheelchair. Rebeka's father, Clarence, is mentally disabled.

Rebeka helps her dad take care of her mom. When Clarence needs a break, Rebeka *has to* cook food for her mom and help her eat. She also *has to help* her use the bathroom. In the evenings when Rebeka *has to do* her homework, she and her mom work on their computers together. They also go to the supermarket together. Shopping for food isn't their favorite activity, but they only *have to go* once a week. When they go, Rebeka *doesn't have to make* a shopping list. Her mom knows exactly what she wants!

Rebeka likes taking care of her mom. "She's taught me how to express myself for who I am and not try to be somebody else," says Rebeka. "Even though she has her disability, . . . she doesn't try to be somebody else, and I [like] that."

Comprehension

3 Write *T* for *true*, *F* for *false*, or *NI* for *no information*.

___T___ 1 Rebeka helps take care of her mother.

_____ 2 Rebeka's mother can't walk.

_____ 3 Rebeka's father is also disabled.

_____ 4 Rebeka is an only child.

_____ 5 Rebeka does all the shopping for the family.

Vocabulary: Household chores

4 [3 26] Listen and repeat. Label the pictures with phrases in the box. Which phrases are not in the pictures?

- clean • ~~cook~~ • do the dishes • do the laundry
- empty the dishwasher • go shopping • iron
- make breakfast/lunch/dinner • make the bed
- set the table • take the garbage out • vacuum
- wash the car

1 *cook*   2 _____   3 _____

4 _____   5 _____   6 _____

7 _____   8 _____   9 _____

💡 Solve it!

5 🎧 ³/₂₇ Listen. What six chores can you hear the person doing? Write them in your notebook.

1 The person is vacuuming.

Grammar

have to/don't have to

Affirmative

I **have to go** to work at 6:00.
She **has to help** her mother.

Negative

I **don't have to do** it.
She **doesn't have to do** all the housework.

Questions	Short form
Do you **have to help**?	Yes, I **do**./No, I **don't**.
Does he **have to do** the laundry?	Yes, he **does**./No, he **doesn't**.
What do they **have to do**?	The dishes.

☛ Go to page 138, Master your grammar.

Practice

6 Complete the article about a teenage caregiver, Ed, with the correct form of *have to* and the verbs in parentheses.

Ed's day is a busy one. He gets up at 6:00. "I ¹ ___*have to start*___ (start) early," he says. "There's a lot to do." First he ² _____ (wake) his mother. Then he ³ _____ (make) breakfast and helps his sister to get ready for school. "Then I ⁴ _____ (do) my newspaper route !" says Ed. "That's OK because I ⁵ _____ (not be) at school until nine o'clock." When he gets home, he ⁶ _____ (do) the laundry and then does his homework. ⁷ _____ (his sister/help) in the house, too? "Yes," says Ed, "but she ⁸ _____ (not do) any cooking or cleaning. She ⁹ _____ (set) the table and empty the dishwasher. She's only eight!"

7 Look at the chart. In your notebook, ask and answer about Polly and her Peruvian pen pal's daily routine. Use the correct form of *(not) have to*.

A: *What time does Polly have to get up?*
B: *She has to get up at 7:15.*

Activity	Polly	Liliana
get up	7:15	6:30
wear school uniform	✗	✓
household chores	make her bed ✓ clean her room ✓ set the table ✓ make breakfast ✗ clean ✗	make breakfast ✓ do the dishes ✓ take the garbage out ✓ do the laundry ✓ iron ✗

Speak

8a PAIRS Ask and answer the questions.

• What chores do you have to do in the house? How often do you do them?
• Which of them do you hate doing?
• What chores don't you have to do? Who does them?
• Do you have any brothers or sisters? If yes, what do they have to do?

b Now tell the class about your partner.

Nadia has to set the table every day . . .

Write

9 On a piece of paper, write about what you have to do in the house and what your brother or sister does/doesn't have to do.

I hate household chores. I have to do a lot, and my little brother doesn't have to do much. For example, . . .

> Extra practice
• Student Book, page 122, Lesson 11B
• Language Builder: WB, page 84; GB, page 136
• Student CD-ROM, Unit 11

I had to call the fire department.

Grammar *had to/didn't have to*
Function Talk about difficult or funny past events

A tricky situation!

Have you ever been in a tricky situation? This week, Kelly from Chicago tells us her story.

Last week I went to my neighbors' house to babysit for their daughter, Lara. I **had to play** with her, read her a story, and put her to bed. I **didn't have to cook** dinner or anything. Before bedtime, Lara went into the bathroom. Then she shouted, "Kelly! I can't get out!" I tried to open the door, but the door handle broke! Lara's parents were at the theater and their cell phone was switched off. Finally, I **had to call** the fire department, and they opened the bathroom door.

Get started

1 Look at the picture. What do you think is happening?

Read

2 🎧 3 28 Listen and read along. What is the "tricky situation"? _____

Comprehension

3 Answer the questions.

1 Where was Kelly last week?

2 Why did Kelly go there?

3 What did Kelly and Lara do together before bedtime?

4 What happened when Kelly tried to open the door?

5 Who opened the door?

Grammar

had to/didn't have to	
Affirmative	
She **had to play** with Lara.	
Negative	
She **didn't have to cook** dinner.	
Questions	
Did she **have to call** the fire department?	
Short answers	
Yes, she **did**./No, she **didn't**.	

☛ Go to page 138, Master your grammar.

Practice

4 Complete Greg's e-mail with *had to* or *didn't have to* and the words in the box.

> • buy • eat • ~~go back~~ • pay • stay • walk

```
Inbox                                           [_][□][×]
File  Edit  View  Go  Tools  Actions  Help
Reply   Reply All   Forward →

Hi Johnny!

I got back home this morning. What a crazy vacation!
First, my sister forgot her passport, so we
1 _____had to go back_____ for it. Then we
went to the wrong airport terminal, so we
2 _____ to the right one.
After that, the airline canceled our flight, so we
3 _____ in an airport hotel
for the night, but luckily we
4 _____ for it. Finally,
we arrived. There was fish for dinner every night.
Luckily, I 5 _____ it because
there were other things. Then on the last day, my
brother Toby dropped his phone in the sea, and
he 6 _____ a new one.
He was not pleased!

Write soon,

Greg
```

5 Ask Greg questions. Then answer.

1 you go back/for your sister's passport?

You: *Did you have to go back for your sister's passport?*

Greg: *Yes, we did.*

2 your parents/pay/for the airport hotel?

_____

_____

3 you/eat/the fish?

_____

_____

4 Toby/buy/a new phone?

_____

_____

Pronunciation: Word stress in two-syllable words

6 Go to page 127.

Listen

7 🎧 3/31 Listen to the conversation and number the pictures in order.

Speak

8 **PAIRS** Talk about a difficult or funny situation. What did you have to do? Use the cues below.

I forgot to do my math homework yesterday.
I had to do it on the bus on the way to school!

- you forgot to do something
- you locked yourself out of your house
- you broke something   • you forgot a birthday

Write

9 On a piece of paper, write a paragraph about a situation that your partner told you about in Exercise 8. Use *had to/didn't have to*.

Joaquin forgot to meet his friend at the movie theater. She had to watch the movie alone! He . . .

> **> Extra practice**
> - **Student Book, page 123, Lesson 11C**
> - **Language Builder: WB, page 86; GB, page 137**
> - **Student CD-ROM, Unit 11**

Curriculum link: Health

Get started

1 Look at the photos. The people are getting *first aid*. What is *first aid*?

Read

Learning strategy: Skim for gist

When you want to get an idea of what a text is about, you can skim it. Look at the headings in the text. Then read quickly and look for key words.

2 Look at the headings (a–e) below, then skim the first aid tips 1–5. Label the tips with the correct headings. Then read again, more slowly. Check your answers.

a) How to treat a cut finger
b) How to treat a sprained ankle
c) How to treat a minor burn on your hand
d) How to treat a nosebleed
e) How to treat someone who has fainted

New words and phrases
- first aid • treat (v) • cut
- sprained • burn (n)
- nosebleed • faint(ed)
- squeeze • ice pack • wash
- wrap • bleeding • remove
- dirt • antiseptic • bandage
- lift (v) • ground • frozen
- swelling • disappear(ed)
- loosen • throw
- running water • cover (v)

---

www.health4all.co.net

File Edit View Favorites Tools Help

First aid

If you have an accident at home or somebody is sick, do you know what you should do? You don't have to be a doctor, but it helps to know something about first aid. Check out the tips below.

First aid tips

1 _How to treat a nosebleed_
- Sit down and put your head between your knees.
- Squeeze your nose with your finger and thumb for five minutes.
- Put an ice pack on your nose.

2 _____
- Wash the finger under the tap to remove any dirt.
- Wrap a paper towel around the finger to stop the bleeding.
- Put some antiseptic cream on the cut.
- Put a bandage on the finger.

3 _____
- Lift the ankle off the ground.
- Put an ice pack or a bag of frozen peas on the ankle for 15 minutes.
- When the swelling disappears, put a bandage around the ankle.

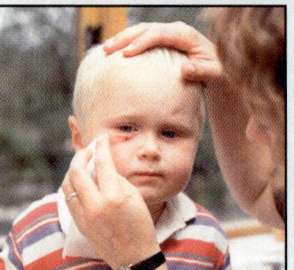
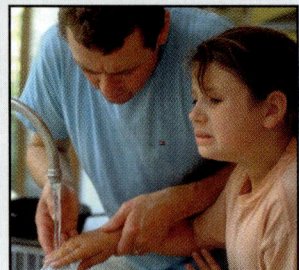

4 _____
- Lift the person's legs off the ground a little.
- Loosen any tight clothes.
- Open the window.
- Don't throw water on the face.

5 _____
- Put the hand under a tap of cold running water.
- Cover the burn with a bandage.
- Take a painkiller if the burn hurts.

Comprehension

3a Match the first aid tips from the website on page 100 to the pictures below.

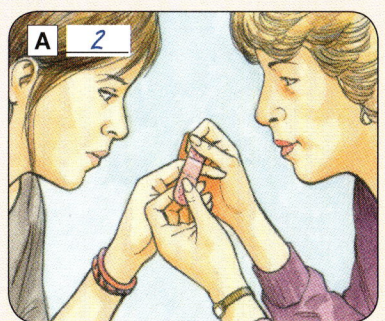 A _2_

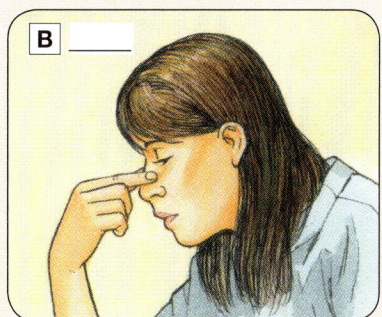 B ____

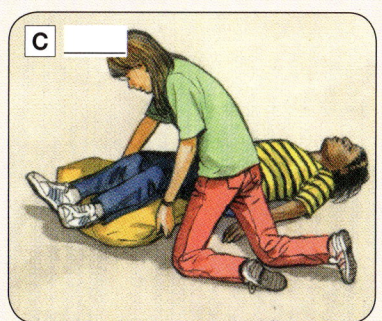 C ____

 D ____

 E ____

b Check (✓) the boxes to show which treatments are correct for the situations.

Treatment	a nosebleed	a cut	a sprained ankle	fainting	a burn
1 Wash with warm water.		✓			✓
2 Cover with a bandage.					
3 Lift the foot or feet off the ground.					
4 Use an ice pack.					
5 Make sure the clothes aren't tight.					

Listen

4 🎧 3/32 Listen to a program about accidents in the home. Answer the questions.

1 Why was Kathryn in the kitchen?
   She was making lunch.
2 What was in the oven?
   _____
3 What "stupid" thing did Kathryn do?
   _____
4 What was the result?
   _____
5 What did she do to take the pain away?
   _____

Speak

5 PAIRS Ask and answer the questions.
• Have you ever had an accident in the home?
• What happened?

Write

6 Someone posts this question on the health4all website. Write your advice on a piece of paper. Use the first aid tips on page 100 to help you.

> _Question_
> _My sister fainted last week, and I just put her on a chair. Was that right? If it happens again, what I should do?_
> _Jenna_

I'm sorry to hear about your sister. If it happens again, this is what you should do . . .

CLIL PROJECT, page 140

To help the environment

Action

12

Grammar	Infinitives of purpose
Vocabulary	Containers and materials
Function	Talk about the environment

Get started

1 The *environment* is the land, water, and air we live in. Does the environment need our help? Why or why not?

Presentation

2 🎧 ³³ Listen and read along. What does Lin want to do next? Why?

Lin and her family are going back to Canada soon. Greg is helping Lin to recycle some of her things before she goes.

Dad: OK, guys, I need your help **to lift** the boxes and bags out of the trunk.

Greg: No problem. I'll take the magazines.

Dad: OK. That's everything. I'm just going to the gas station **to get** some gas.

Greg: OK. Lin, you do the bottles, and I'll do the magazines.

Lin: Oh, no! My beautiful magazines. I don't want to throw them away.

Greg: We aren't throwing them away. We're recycling them **to help** the environment. Anyway, you can't take them back to Canada.

Lin: Yes, that's true. OK, so where do glass bottles go? In the green bin?

Greg: No! That's for yard waste—plants and stuff. The blue bin is for glass, metal, paper, and plastic.

Lin: OK . . . Hey, after this, can we go to the store **to buy** a magazine? I don't have any left!

Comprehension

3 Correct the sentences.

                    boxes and bags
1 There are some ~~suitcases~~ in the trunk of the car.

2 Lin's father is going to the supermarket.

3 Lin and Greg are going to recycle some clothes.

4 Glass goes in the green bin.

5 Lin wants to buy a newspaper.

💡 Solve it!

4 Look at the photo on page 102. Circle the bin for yard waste.

Vocabulary: Containers and materials

5a 🎧 3/34 Listen and repeat. Say what containers are in pictures 1–7 below. Then match the pictures to the material and container words.

> **Containers**
> __ bag __ bottle *1* box __ can __ carton
> __ jar __ packet
>
> **Materials**
> *1* cardboard __ glass __ metal __ paper
> __ plastic

b Name five containers and their contents that are in your kitchen at home.

Grammar

> **Infinitives of purpose**
>
> I need your help **to lift** these boxes and bags.
>
> I'm going to the gas station **to get** some gas.

☛ Go to page 139, Master your grammar.

Practice

6 In your notebook, rewrite each question below with an infinitive of purpose.

1 After you use a computer or watch TV, do you turn it off to save electricity?

> ### Quiz: How green are you?
>
> **Put a check (✓) if the answer is "Yes." Put a cross (✗) if the answer is "No."**
>
> **1 Saving electricity**
> After you use a computer or watch TV, do you turn it off? ☐
>
> **2 Saving water**
> Do you take showers, not baths? ☐
>
> **3 Recycling your trash**
> Do you have separate bins in your kitchen? ☐
>
> **4 Helping the environment**
> When you go shopping, do you reuse old plastic bags? ☐
>
> **5 Saving gas**
> Do you walk or bike into town rather than ask your parents for a ride? ☐
>
> **6 Making sure you eat healthily**
> Do you usually eat fruit and vegetables each day? ☐

Speak

7 **PAIRS** Ask and answer the questions in the quiz above.

Listen

8 🎧 3/35 Martin is buying a cell phone. Listen. Complete the sentences with infinitives of purpose.

1 Charities look at the phone __to see if it works__.
2 They use the money _____.
3 You can search the Internet _____.
4 Recycling companies use the plastic _____.
5 They use the metal _____.

Write

9 On a piece of paper, write about four things you can do to help the environment. Use the quiz in Exercise 6 to help you.

> **Extra practice**
> • **Student Book, page 123, Lesson 12A**
> • **Language Builder: WB, page 90; GB, page 140**
> • **Student CD-ROM, Unit 12**

Grammar	*so* + adjective + *that*
Vocabulary	Wild animals and insects
Function	Talk about animals and insects

Get started

1 Look at the photo of the shark. What words does it make you think of?

dangerous, . . .

Read

2 Listen and read along. How many sharks did people kill last year? _____

Comprehension

3 Write *T* for *true*, *F* for *false*, or *NI* for *no information*.

___F__ 1 People love sharks more than dolphins.
_____ 2 Ninety percent of sharks are not dangerous.
_____ 3 Sharks kill a lot of people every year.
_____ 4 Humans usually kill sharks for sport.
_____ 5 People pay a lot for shark fin soup.

Solve it!

4 Look at the ad again. What does "SOS" stand for?

SHARKS
DANGEROUS OR IN DANGER?

SOS

Some people are **so** scared of sharks **that** they don't swim in the sea. They think sharks are cruel and dangerous. People don't love sharks in the way that they love dolphins, whales, elephants, and tigers.

But sharks are in danger. Here are the facts.
- There are 390 types of sharks, but only 10% are dangerous.
- Sharks are **so** intelligent **that** they rarely attack humans. They don't like the taste.
- Last year, sharks killed 4 people around the world.
- Last year, humans killed around 100 million sharks.

People usually kill sharks for their fins. Shark fin soup is a popular and expensive dish in many Chinese restaurants. In fact, it is **so** popular and expensive **that** sharks are now in danger.

Take action to protect sharks.
Join Save Our Sharks today!

Shark fins

Vocabulary: Wild animals and insects

5 🎧 ³⁷ Listen and repeat. Then match the pictures above to the words in the box below. Which words are not in the pictures?

> ___ ant ___ cheetah ___ chimpanzee
> ___ crocodile ___ dolphin ___ elephant ___ fly
> ___ giraffe ___ gorilla ___ hippo ___ leopard
> ___ lion ___ monkey ___ mosquito _1_ rhino
> ___ snake ___ shark ___ spider ___ tiger
> ___ wasp ___ whale ___ zebra

Speak

6 **PAIRS** Which animal or insect is:
a) the most beautiful?   b) the most dangerous?
c) the fastest?   d) the heaviest?   e) the scariest?

Grammar

so + adjective + *that*

Some people are **so** scared of sharks **that** they don't swim in the sea.

Shark fin soup is **so** popular and expensive **that** sharks are now in danger.

☛ Go to page 139, Master your grammar.

2B

Practice

7 Complete the text with *so . . . that* and words from the box.

> • interesting • scared • ~~intelligent~~
> • difficult • similar to humans

Chimps

Chimpanzees are ¹ _so intelligent that_ they can use tools. And they are ² _____ a lot of scientists want to study them. When Dr. Jane Goodall first arrived in their jungle, the chimps were ³ _____ they didn't come near her. Her job was ⁴ _____ she almost went home. But chimpanzees are ⁵ _____ she stayed and wrote 12 books about them.

Write

8 On a piece of paper, write the text for a new poster for the SPS (Snake Protection Society). Use the information below and the ad about sharks to help you.

Some people are so scared of snakes that they run away from them . . .

FACTFILE Snakes

SNAKE PROTECTION SOCIETY

- People are scared—they run away from snakes.
- People think snakes are cruel and dangerous.
- There are about 2,500 types of snake.
- Only 20% are poisonous.
- People kill millions of snakes every year for their skin (snakeskin bags and shoes = popular and expensive).
- Many species of snakes are now in danger.

 Extra practice
- **Student Book, page 123, Lesson 12B**
- **Language Builder: WB, page 92; GB, page 140**
- **Student CD-ROM, Unit 12**

105

Grammar   *would ('d) rather*
             would ('d) prefer
Function   Say good-bye

Get started

1 What is an *adventure course*? Would you like to go on one?

Presentation

2 [3 38] Listen and read along. What does Lin think of the adventure course?

Polly: Wow! It's a real adventure course! It looks awesome!

Lin: Awesome? It looks scary!

Greg: Come on. It's your last weekend. Let's all give it a try.

Polly: Well, I'm up for it. What about you, Lin?

Lin: Sorry! No way! **I'd rather jump** in a cold bath than go up there! It's too high!

Greg: Don't be such a wimp! It isn't dangerous.

Lin: No, honestly. **I'd prefer to stand** and watch.

Polly: Are you sure? **Would** you **rather go** canoeing? We can do that instead.

Lin: And fall in the river? No, I wouldn't, thanks.

Carlos: Actually, I think I'll stay with Lin . . . um . . . so she's not alone.

Greg: OK. See you later, guys. Come on, Polly.

Phrases

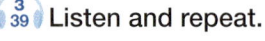

[3 39] Listen and repeat.

• give it a try. • up for it. • It looks awesome!
• Don't be such a wimp!

Comprehension

3 Answer the questions.

1 What is the adventure course like?
2 Who wants to do it?
3 What does Lin want to do?
4 Who stays with Lin? Why?

Grammar

would ('d) rather/would ('d) prefer

Affirmative

I**'d rather jump** in a cold bath **than go** up there.
I**'d prefer to stand** and **watch**.

Negative

I**'d rather not walk** along that.
I**'d prefer not to go** on that.

Questions	Short answers
Would you **rather try** the course **or watch**?	**Watch**.
Would you **rather go** canoeing?	Yes, I **would**./ No, I **wouldn't**.
Would you **prefer to go** canoeing?	

☛ Go to page 139, Master your grammar.

Practice

4a In your notebook, write sentences with *'d rather* and *'d prefer to* and the cues.

1 go to the sports center ✗ /go to the beach ✓
I'd rather not go to the sports center.
I'd prefer to go to the beach.
2 have a barbecue ✗ /have a picnic ✓
3 play football ✗ /play a video game ✓
4 stay at home ✗ /go into town ✓
5 watch a DVD ✗ /go to the movies ✓

b Make other sentences from the cues, using *I'd rather . . . than.*

I'd rather go to the sports center than go to the beach.

Pronunciation: Sentence stress

5 🎧 Go to page 127.

Use your English: Say good-bye

6 🎧 ³/₄₂ **PAIRS** Listen and repeat. Then practice the conversation.

Greg: Have a safe trip back to Canada, Lin!
Lin: Thanks.
Carlos: And don't forget to send us an e-mail.
Lin: No, I won't. Take care, Polly.
Polly: Yes, I will. See you next year.
Lin: Yes, I hope so. Bye!

Say good-bye	
Parting remarks	**Responses**
• Have a good/safe trip!	• Thanks.
• Have a great vacation!	• Thanks. You, too.
• Take care.	• Yes, I will.
• Don't forget to call/ e-mail/text me.	• No, I won't.
• See you soon!	• Yes, I hope so.

7 **PAIRS** Role-play similar "good-bye" conversations.

Write

8 Look at the list of activities. On a piece of paper, write about the activities you would rather do or prefer to do and why.

• visit Europe/the U.S.?   • exercise/surf the Internet?
• read/watch TV?   • spend time with friends?

I'd rather visit Europe than visit the U.S. because I love old cities . . .

> **Extra practice**
> • **Student Book, page 123, Lesson 12C**
> • **Language Builder: WB, page 94; GB, page 141**
> • **Student CD-ROM, Unit 12**

Before you read, go to page 109.

Values for living

Teen Zine Problem Page

Dear Teen Zine

I have a problem, and I hope you can help.

My best friend is named Jacob. We're very close, but we're also very different. Jacob's passion is animals. He's a vegetarian, and last year he did a 5-mile run to raise money for the animal charity WWF.* I like animals, too, but my real passion is clothes. Jacob says, "Sasha's passion is fashion!"

A few weeks ago, I went into town, and a woman stopped me in the street. She was a scout for a model agency. I went to the agency with my mom the next week. They took some photos, and I got an interview for a modeling job almost immediately.

When I arrived at the interview, they wanted to take some test photographs. They gave me some clothes to wear. There was a fur jacket and some other clothes with animal fur. I was so excited that I didn't think about the fur. Two days later they offered me the job!

Sasha and Jacob

When I told Jacob about it, he was so angry that he walked out of the room. He says that I shouldn't take the job because they want me to wear animal fur, and he thinks that wearing fur is cruel. I really want to be a model—modeling is my dream job— but I don't want to lose my best friend. Please help!

Sasha Winters

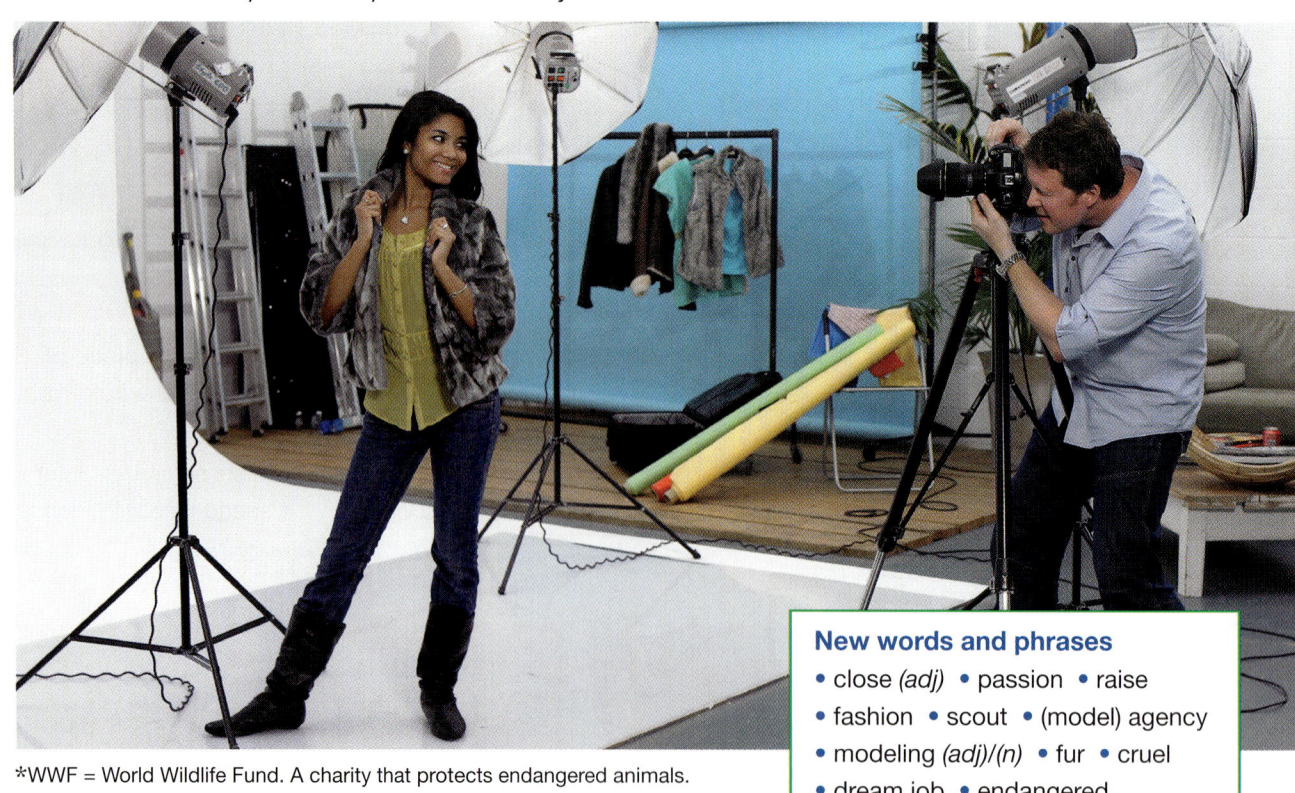

*WWF = World Wildlife Fund. A charity that protects endangered animals.

New words and phrases
• close *(adj)* • passion • raise
• fashion • scout • (model) agency
• modeling *(adj)/(n)* • fur • cruel
• dream job • endangered

Get started

1 What is a "Problem Page"? Have you ever written to a Problem Page to ask for advice?

Read

2 Read the letter on page 108. What is Sasha's problem? _____

Comprehension

3 Correct the mistakes.

animals
1 Jacob loves ~~clothes~~.

2 Jacob raised money for his school last year.

3 A woman stopped Jacob in the street.

4 Sasha got her first interview after a long time.

5 The fashion company never uses animal fur.

Speak your mind!

> **Learning strategy: Be a good listener!**
> While you listen, smile, nod your head, and say things like "OK," "Sure," "I see," "Really?"

4a **PAIRS** Read the quotes below. Then say who you agree with and why.

I agree with Eduardo because wearing fur is cruel to animals.

> Wearing animal fur is wrong. It's really cruel to kill animals for their fur, and Sasha shouldn't take the job.

Eduardo, 16

> There's nothing wrong with animal fur. We wear leather shoes and jackets. What's the difference?

Alina, 16

> Some animal fur is OK—rabbit fur, for example. Sasha should find out which animal the fur is from.

Bettina, 15

> It's Sasha's decision. Jacob should support his friend.

Gordon, 16

b Now, say what Sasha should do.

A: *I think Sasha should take the job because it's really important for her future.*

B: *Really? I think . . .*

Listen

5a 🔊 3/43 Listen to Sasha talking to Tanya from the modeling agency. What is the solution to Sasha's problem? _____

b 🔊 3/43 Listen again. In your notebook, complete Sasha's notes below.

> *Phone call with Tanya Burgess at*
> *One World Modeling Agency.*
> *New interview with* ¹_____ *Fashions*
> *at* ²_____ *o'clock on* ³_____
> *Address:* ⁴_____ *Street*
> *Phone number:* ⁵_____

Write

6a Read this letter from a Problem Page.

> ### Dear Teen Zine,
>
> My uncle gave me a snakeskin belt for my birthday. It's a beautiful belt, but I don't believe in killing animals for fashion. I'm going to see my uncle next weekend. What should I do?
>
> **Sergio**

b Now write an answer on a piece of paper. Tell Sergio what you think he should do.

Dear Sergio,

I'm sorry to hear about your problem. Why don't you . . . . If that doesn't work, perhaps you should . . . . Remember, it's always important to . . . . I hope my advice helps, and good luck!

CLIL PROJECT, page 140

Grammar (40 points)

1 Write one sentence with *should* and one sentence with *shouldn't*. (8 points)

0 I'm really tired. (go to bed/watch TV)
You should go to bed. You shouldn't watch TV!

1 She doesn't feel well. (go home/stay at school)
_____

2 My computer is broken. (fix it/throw it out)
_____

3 They're very heavy. (sit on the sofa/exercise)
_____

4 Ed has a stomachache. (eat so fast/drink some water)
_____

2 Complete the conversation with the correct form of *have to* or *had to*. (8 points)

Sara: What a busy day I had yesterday!
         I ⁰ _____*had to*_____ do a lot of chores in the house.

Emma: What ¹ _____ you
         _____ do?

Sara: I ² _____ clean my
         room, cook, vacuum, and do the dishes.
         Luckily, I ³ _____ do
         the laundry because my mom did it.
         ⁴ _____ you _____ do
         housework every day?

Emma: Yes, I do, because my mom
         ⁵ _____ go to work. But I
         ⁶ _____ do everything.
         My dad does the shopping.
         ⁷ _____ your little brother
         _____ do any housework?

Sara: No, he doesn't. He
         ⁸ _____ do anything!

3 Write sentences with infinitives of purpose. (5 points)

0 I'm going to the store. We need to buy some milk.
I'm going to the store to buy some milk.

1 Inez reads English books. She wants to practice English.
_____

2 George works a lot. He needs to save money.
_____

3 I go to the gym. I want to be thin.
_____

4 We take showers. We want to save water.
_____

5 You should recycle. It helps the environment.
_____

4 Complete the sentences using *so + that*. (10 points)

0 I was _____*so hungry that*_____ (hungry) I ate six sandwiches!
1 Mia was _____ (scared) she ran away.
2 The class was _____ (boring) I fell asleep.
3 Giraffes are _____ (tall) they can eat tree leaves.
4 The homework was _____ (hard) I couldn't finish it.
5 Rhinos are _____ (strong) they can move cars.

5 Complete the sentences with *would rather (not)* or *would prefer (not to)*. (9 points)

0 I/rather/eat pizza. (✗) _____*I'd rather not eat pizza.*_____
1 Let's not play games. I/prefer/listen to music. (✓)
_____

2 you/rather/stay at home or go out (?)
_____

3 I/rather/watch this show. It's awful! (✗)
_____

4 I/prefer/do my homework on my laptop. (✓)
_____

5 I/rather/stay at home tomorrow. (✓)
_____

6 you/rather/go to the park or the beach (?)
_____

7 I/prefer/go on that roller coaster. It looks scary! (✗)
_____

8 What/you/prefer/do (?)
_____

9 I/rather/go in the water. It's freezing today! (✗)
_____

Vocabulary (40 points)

6 Complete the sentences. (8 points)

0 I ate too much candy. I have a ___*toothache*___ .

1 Do you have a painkiller? I have a _____ .

2 I have a _____ . I think that food was bad.

3 I have a _____ in my leg.

4 Ouch! My arm _____ .

5 I got some water in my ear. Now I have an

_____ .

6 I can't eat any chips. I have a sore _____ .

7 That's a bad _____ . Try some hot lemon.

8 When you have the flu, you get a high _____ .

7 Complete with chores. (12 points)

0 I washed the clothes. Let's _____*iron*_____ them.

1 Dinner's nearly ready. Can you _____ the
table?

2 Could you help me to _____ breakfast?

3 We need some food. Can you go _____ ?

4 The kitchen looks awful. Take the _____ out.

5 My jeans are dirty. I need to do the _____ .

6 The plates are dirty. Can you do the _____ ?

7 My dad _____ dinner every night.

8 I want you to _____ your room. It's a mess!

9 The carpet is dirty. Can you _____ ?

10 Dad is going to give me $5 if I _____ his car.

11 Can you empty the _____ , please?

12 It's 12:00. Can you help me to make _____ ?

8 Complete the material and container words.
Use one word twice. (10 points)

0 a m_e_ _t_ _a_ l c_a_ n

1 a pl_____c b_t_____

2 a c___d__o____d b___

3 a g_____s j___

4 a p_____r b___

5 a c_____d c___t_n

9 Put the animals into the groups. (10 points)

> • ant • cheetah • dolphin • fly • leopard
> • mosquito • rhino • shark • tiger • whale • zebra

Insect	Has four legs	Lives in water
	cheetah	

Use your English (20 points)

10 Choose the correct answer. (8 points)

0 **A:** You a) don't feel well. b) (don't look very well.)
c) 're well.   Are you OK?

1 **B:** No, I'm not. I a) feel sick.   b) don't feel bad.
c) take medicine.

2 **A:** What's a) the illness? b) the matter? c) matter?

3 **B:** I ate some chocolate and now I a) feel
b) get c) have a stomachache.

4 **A:** Oh, no! a) That's too bad! b) You're sad!
c) Very sick!

5 You a) must be b) will be   c) should go home

6 **B:** Yes, a) you're a friend. b) you're right.
c) you're a good idea.

7 **A:** OK. Bye for now. a) Take care!
b) Look at yourself! c) Care yourself!

8 **B:** I will. a) Have you b) You're having
c) Have a great vacation!

11 Complete B's part in each mini-conversation
with a phrase from the box. (12 points)

> • give it a try? • cost a ton! • With a little luck,
> • I hate to say this, but • Don't be such a wimp!
> • up for it! • looks awesome!

0 **A:** I'm really scared of swimming in the sea.
  B: ___*Don't be such a wimp!*___

1 **A:** Oh, no! It's still raining.
  B: _____ it will stop soon and
  we can go out.

2 **A:** What do you think of Jack's new bike?
  B: It _____

3 **A:** Wow! That's a fantastic laptop!
  B: It's my Dad's. It _____

4 **A:** Would you like to go windsurfing later?
  B: Well, I've never tried, but I'm _____

5 **A:** That's a cool computer game!
  B: Would you like to _____

6 **A:** I'm so happy we finished all our tests!
  B: Well, _____ we have a
  math test tomorrow!

SELF-CHECK	
Grammar	____ /40
Vocabulary	____ /40
Use your English	____ /20
Total score	____ /100

Extra practice

Unit 1

Lesson 1A, Grammar

Make sentences in the simple present.

1 His parents (be from ✗) Seattle.
   His parents aren't from Seattle.

2 I (live ✗) in the U.K. I (live ✓) in the U.S.
   _____

3 A: they (speak) Italian?   B: No, they (do ✗).
   _____

4 She (work ✗) in a bank. She (work ✓) in a school.
   _____

5 A: she (live) here now?   B: Yes, she (do).
   _____

6 John (speak ✓) English, but (speak ✗) French.
   _____

7 A: (you/like) your teacher?   B: Yes, I (do).
   _____

8 We (like ✗) New York. We (like ✓) Florida.
   _____

Vocabulary: Family

Look at the family tree. Write sentences.

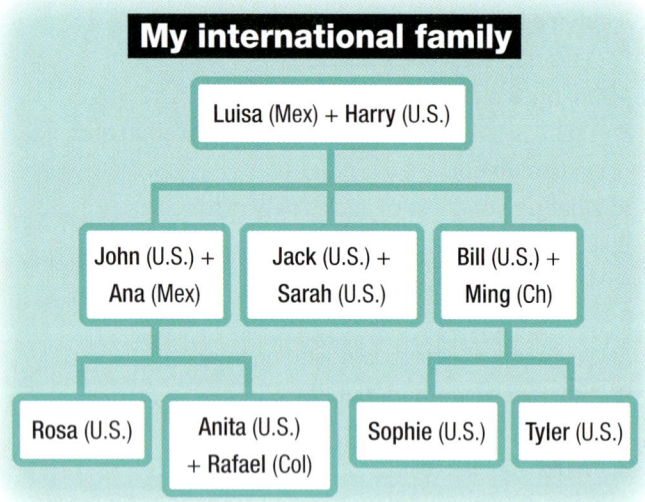

1 Ana/John: *Ana is John's wife. She's Mexican.*
2 Sarah/Rosa: _____
3 Sophie and Tyler/Anita: _____
   _____
4 Ming/Sophie and Tyler: _____
   _____
5 Harry/Sophie: _____
6 Rafael/Anita: _____

Lesson 1B, Grammar

1 Write sentences about Simon's day.

Simon gets up at 7 o'clock. _____

2 Make sentences with expressions of frequency.

1 I/have/a snack in the morning. (usually)
   I usually have a snack in the morning.

2 My mother/have/breakfast in bed. (never)
   _____

3 they/eat/dinner together? (How often)
   _____

4 Carlos/be/late for school. (sometimes)
   _____

5 your sister/exercise? (How often)
   _____

6 My brother/play/soccer. (once a week)
   _____

7 My grandfather/rest in the afternoon. (usually)
   _____

8 We/take a break/at 11 A.M. (always)
   _____

Lesson 1C, Grammar

1 Write questions and answers. It's midday in New York. Look at the box below. What are the people doing now?

---
1 **Brazil 2 P.M.** Alonzo / eat lunch
2 **California 9 A.M.** Hilary / get up
3 **Japan 3 A.M.** Kaori / sleep
4 **Spain 6 P.M.** Pedro and Inez / come home from work
---

1 A: *What is Alonzo doing?*
  B: *He's eating lunch.*
  A: *Why? What time is it in Brazil?*
  B: *It's 2 P.M.*
2 A: _____
  B: _____
  A: _____
  B: _____
3 A: _____
  B: _____
  A: _____
  B: _____
4 A: _____
  B: _____
  A: _____
  B: _____

2 Write sentences in the present continuous. The weather's very bad today. What is everyone doing?

1 I/not swim today. (with my friend online)
I'm not swimming today. I'm chatting with my friend online.
2 They/not play/football. (music)
_____
_____
3 Lara/not have/a tennis lesson. (the net)
_____
_____
4 Jimmy/not play basketball. (guitar)
_____
_____
5 Luz and I/not shop. (with friends)
_____
_____
6 Selina's parents/not work. (their books)
_____
_____

Unit 2

Lesson 2A, Vocabulary: Jobs

Write the correct ending to complete the job words. Then put them in the puzzle and find job number 12.

1 mech *anic*   2 polit_____   3 pi_____   4 car_____
5 detec_____   6 direc_____   7 engin_____   8 den_____
9 cash_____   10 taxi dri_____   11 journa_____

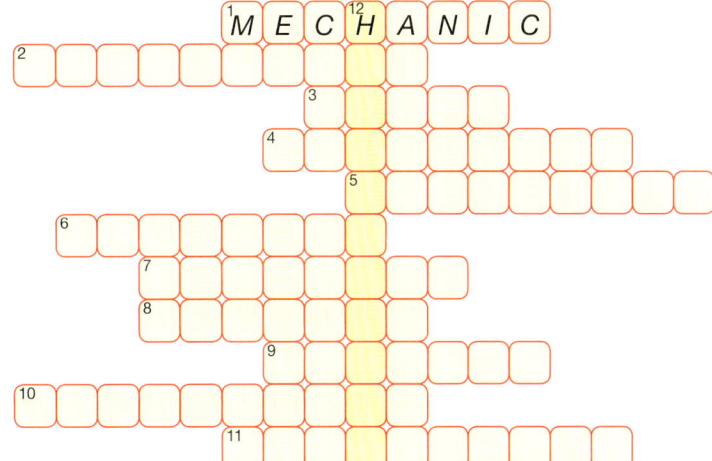

Grammar

Complete the conversation. Use the simple present or present continuous forms of the verbs.

John: What [1] _____ *does your father do* _____ (your father/do)?
Miriam: He's a taxi driver. He [2] _____ (drive) people all over New York.
John: [3] _____ (he/work) right now?
Miriam: Yes, he is. He [4] _____ (drive) a woman to the airport.
John: [5] _____ (he/always work) on Sunday?
Miriam: No, he [6] _____ (not), but he [7] _____ (work) today because he [8] _____ (want) a free day tomorrow. It's his birthday.

Lesson 2B, Vocabulary: Everyday objects

Find the differences! Look at the pictures of Vicky and Dave. There are eight differences between the two pictures. Write them in your notebook.

1 In Picture A she has a necklace. In Picture B she doesn't.

Grammar

Rewrite the sentences with the verb *be* and possessive pronouns.

1 The watch belongs to her husband.
  The watch is his.

2 This DVD belongs to me and my brother.
  _____

3 That necklace belongs to me.
  _____

4 That new laptop belongs to my boyfriend.
  _____

5 The house belongs to my parents.
  _____

6 This pen belongs to you!
  _____

7 That bracelet belongs to my grandmother.
  _____

Lesson 2C, Vocabulary: Food and drink

Find twelve food words in this wordsearch.

Grammar

Complete the conversation with *there's, there are, is there,* or *are there*.

Polly: Let's make an omelette. ¹ *Are there* any eggs in the fridge?

Carlos: Yes, ² _____ . ³ _____ four. And ⁴ _____ some salt and pepper here. What else do we need?

Polly: ⁵ _____ any cheese?

Carlos: No, I'm sorry, ⁶ _____ no cheese.

Polly: OK. ⁷ _____ any tomatoes?

Carlos: Yes, ⁸ _____ , and ⁹ _____ some onions, too.

Unit 3
Lesson 3A, Grammar

Complete the sentences in Lin's e-mail with the correct forms of the verbs in parentheses.

File Edit View Go Tools Actions Help
Reply 📩 Reply All 📩 Forward ➥

Hi, Susie!
Well, I'm here in Seattle now. I like my cousin Polly because we ¹ _*enjoy doing*_ (enjoy/do) the same things. I also have some new friends named Carlos and Greg. Carlos is very good at computers, and he ² _____ (not mind/help) me. Greg's really nice, too. He ³ _____ (like/play) basketball, and he ⁴ _____ (love/go) skateboarding. His brother Toby is 18, and he's really cool. He ⁵ _____ (prefer/play) soccer. I ⁶ _____ (enjoy/do) gymnastics once a week, and Polly ⁷ _____ (like/do) karate. She prefers indoor sports because she ⁸ _____ (not like/get) cold! Write soon!
Love, Lin

💡 Solve it!

Find the sports-related word.

1 is in *meat* but it isn't in *meet*   *A*

2 is in *seat* and also in *feet*   _____

3 is in *home* and also in *help*   _____

4 is in *will* and also in *tell*   _____

5 is in *bell* but nowhere in *ball*   _____

6 is in *table*; it's also in *tall*   _____

7 is in *hit* but isn't in *he*   _____

8 is the letter that comes after *b*   _____

Lesson 3B, Grammar

Complete with affirmative or negative imperatives.

A: Mom, where's my Gameboy?

B: ¹ _*Don't play*_ (play) a game now! It's dinnertime.

A: OK. But please ² _____ (tell) me . . . Where's my Gameboy?

B: I'm not sure . . . ³ _____ (look) in your backpack.

A: Oh, here it is. Thanks. . . . Hey, are we having pasta for dinner? ⁴ _____ (put) any cheese on it! I hate cheese!

B: I know. Now, ⁵ _____ (wash) your hands. Then ⁶ _____ (get) a drink for yourself and ⁷ _____ (sit) down at the table.

A: OK, Mom.

Lesson 3C, Grammar

Complete the e-mail. Use the verbs in the box and *be going to*.

> • be • come • ~~do~~ • fly • miss
> • swim • take • visit

```
File  Edit  View  Go  Tools  Actions  Help
Reply 🖂   Reply All 🖂   Forward ➪

Dear Jian,

What ¹ _are_ you _going to do_ this summer?
I ² _____ my grandparents in Florida.
My brother ³ _____, too. My
grandparents ⁴ _____ us to Disneyworld!
We ⁵ _____ at the beach, too. We
⁶ _____ home two days before school
starts. It ⁷ _____ so cool! But
I ⁸ _____ all my friends.

Write soon! Consuelo
```

Unit 4

Lesson 4A, Vocabulary: Home and furniture

Look at the picture and complete the words.

1 ch_imney_   2 bo_____
3 ba_____   4 be_____
5 g_____   6 si_____
7 st_____   8 f_____
9 b_____

Grammar

Complete the conversation with the correct form of the adjectives.

A: Our new house is ¹ _____ (good) than our old house.

B: Great! Where is it?

A: It's in the center of town, but it's ² _____ (far) from school than our other house.

B: What's your favorite room?

A: The attic is ³ _____ (good) room in the house!

B: Cool! Is your bedroom ⁴ _____ (small) or
⁵ _____ (big) than your sister's?

A: That's ⁶ _____ (bad) thing about our new house. Her room is ⁷ _____ (comfortable), and it has ⁸ _____ (large) windows.

B: Maybe you can put your bed in the attic!

Lesson 4B, Grammar

Describe each picture using the cue and *a lot of, a few, a little, many,* or *much*.

1 He has _____ _a lot of_ _____ luggage.
2 There isn't _____ food on his plate.
3 There aren't _____ chairs in the classroom.
4 She only has _____ money in her purse.
5 She has _____ pens on her desk.
6 There isn't _____ luggage on the luggage rack.

Use your English

Match the questions to the pictures above.

a) Excuse me, is it OK if I use one of your pens?

b) Can I have more french fries, please?

c) Can I borrow $10, please?

d) Excuse me, can I put my bags here?

e) Is it OK if I borrow some chairs?

f) Can I take this luggage on the plane?

115

Lesson 4C, Grammar

Complete each question with a word from the box. Then answer the questions.

> • deep • farther • ~~high~~ • smallest • longest
> • taller • weigh • wide

Quick Quiz

1. How ____high____ is Mount Everest? (29,028 ft)
2. Which is the _____ river in the world? (the Nile)
3. How _____ is the Pacific Ocean? (36,160 ft)
4. Which building is _____? The Eiffel Tower or the Empire State Building? (the Empire State Building)
5. How _____ is the Amazon River? (30 miles)
6. Which distance is _____ ? London to Paris or London to Edinburgh? (London to Edinburgh)
7. How much does the A380 Airbus _____? (507 tons)
8. Which country is the _____? Russia, the U.S., or the U.K.? (U.K.)

Unit 5

Lesson 5A, Grammar

Complete with forms of the simple past of *be*.

The Jonas Brothers

Q: Where [1] ___were___ the Jonas Brothers born?
A: They [2] _____ born in New Jersey, U.S.
Q: [3] _____ the brothers always in a band together?
A: No. Nick Jonas [4] _____ a solo singer first. But he [5] _____ very successful until he played with his brothers.
Q: [6] _____ their first record *A Little Bit Longer*?
A: No, it [7] _____. Their first record [8] _____ *It's About Time*.
Q: [9] _____ they on the TV show *Hannah Montana*?
A: Yes, they [10] _____. And they [11] _____ in movies like *Night at the Museum*, too.

 Solve it!

Greg's parents were angry because someone was in their basement at Greg's party. Read the information. Who was in their basement?

_____

- There were eight people at the party, four boys (Greg, Carlos, Tom, and Paul) and four girls (Lin, Lucy, Amy, and Polly).
- The boys weren't in the yard.
- Lin, Lucy, and Amy were in the house. Polly was in the yard.
- Greg and Carlos were in the kitchen with one of the girls.
- Lucy wasn't in the kitchen.
- Lin was in the living room with one other person.
- One of the boys was in Greg's bedroom.
- Lucy and Amy weren't in the living room.
- Paul was with Lin.

Lesson 5B, Grammar

Write B's part of the conversations. Write an affirmative sentence (✓), a negative sentence (✗), or a question (?).

1. **A:** They liked the food. (✗ the music)
   B: Yes, but they ___didn't like the music___.
2. **A:** I needed some bread. (✗ any juice)
   B: Yes, but you _____ .
3. **A:** Dan didn't call last night. (? this morning)
   B: _____ he _____ ?
4. **A:** The train stopped in Boston. (✗ New York)
   B: Yes, but it _____ .
5. **A:** Did he arrive before lunch? (✓ at eleven o'clock)
   B: Yes, he _____ .
6. **A:** My cousins didn't stay with us. (? at a hotel)
   B: _____ they _____ ?

Lesson 5C, Grammar

Complete Greg's e-mail. Use the correct simple past form of the verbs in the box.

> • buy • do • get • give • go • ~~happen~~ • have
> • hurry • leave • make • not tell • take

File Edit View Go Tools Actions Help
Reply   Reply All   Forward

Hi, Carlos!

You'll never believe what ¹ _happened_ yesterday. It was Mom's birthday and I ² _____ some surprises for her. I ³ _____ a cup of coffee to her, ⁴ _____ breakfast, ⁵ _____ the dishes, and then ⁶ _____ to the supermarket to do some shopping. She ⁷ _____ me some money, and I ⁸ _____ everything, but then I ⁹ _____ the eggs at the checkout! I ¹⁰ _____ Mom! I ¹¹ _____ back to the supermarket very fast and ¹² _____ the eggs!

See you soon, Greg

 Solve it!

Where did the friends go? Write the letter of the place (a–i) next to the clue (1–4).

1 Polly went by train. It was sunny. She had a pair of shorts and a swimsuit with her. She played volleyball on the sand with her friends. _b_

2 Greg and Lin went by bus. They had tickets. There was music and a lot of people there. They jumped up and shouted. ☐

3 Carlos and his family went by plane. It was very hot. They visited Cancún. ☐

4 The friends walked there at 9 A.M. They had bags. They listened and answered questions. They went home at 3:30. ☐

> **Places**
> a) the swimming pool b) the beach
> c) the U.K. d) school e) the park f) Mexico
> g) a soccer game h) the movies i) a concert

Unit 6

Lesson 6A, Grammar

There was a bank robbery in Houston yesterday morning. Police officer Ted Brown questioned two people to find out what they were doing that morning. Look at the chart and complete the conversation.

	Sid Brook
9:00–10:00	watch TV
10:00–11:30	drive to Houston
11:30–12:30	have a cup of coffee with Carla Watts
	Carla Watts
9:00–10:00	check my e-mails at home
10:00–11:30	do some shopping
11:30–12:30	have a cup of coffee with Sid Brook

Ted: What ¹ _were you doing_ (you/do) yesterday morning, Mr Brook?

Sid: Between 9 and 10, I ² _____.

Ted: ³ _____ (you/still watch) TV between 10 and 11:30?

Sid: ⁴ _____.

Ted: What ⁵ _____ (you/do) between 11:30 and 12:30?

Sid: ⁶ _____.

Ted: What ⁷ _____ (she/wear)?

Sid: She ⁸ _____ (wear) a red sweater and jeans.

Ted: Thank you. Now, Ms. Watts. What were you doing between 9 and 10 yesterday?

Carla: ⁹ _____.

Ted: ¹⁰ _____ (you/still/check) your e-mails between 10 and 11:30?

Carla: ¹¹ _____.

Ted: And between 11:30 and 12:30?

Carla: ¹² _____.

Ted: What ¹³ _____ (you/wear)?

Carla: I ¹⁴ _____ (wear) a green sweater and jeans.

 Solve it!

The police officer wants to ask Sid and Carla more questions. Why?

Lesson 6B, Grammar

Four people were in a bank when some robbers came in. Complete their statements with the correct form of the verb in the simple past or past continuous.

A I ¹_____was listening_____ (listen) to music when the robbers ²_____came_____ (come) into the bank. While they ³_____ (take) the money, I ⁴_____ (stay) under a desk. **Jason Prentice**

B The robbers ⁵_____ (come) in while I ⁶_____ (talk) to the bank manager. They ⁷_____ (wear) black clothes. I ⁸_____ (stay) behind a desk. **Emma Chao**

C I was outside the bank. I ⁹_____ (wait) for my friend when the robbers ¹⁰_____ (arrive). I ¹¹_____ (go) across the street and ¹²_____ (call) the police. **Edward Ellis**

D When I ¹³_____ (see) the robbers, I ¹⁴_____ (take) out some money from the ATM. I ¹⁵_____ (run) out of the bank. **Olivia Diaz**

Vocabulary: Prepositions of location and motion

Complete the sentences with prepositions from the box.

> • across • next to • on • out of • ~~up~~

1 Arturo ran _____up_____ the stairs to the attic.
2 The dog jumped _____ the car window and ran away.
3 Jenny and Ned are neighbors—they live _____ each other.
4 The laptop is _____ the desk.
5 We walked _____ the bridge to the other side of the river.

Lesson 6C, Grammar

Complete the sentences with *who*, *that*, or *where*.

Alice in Wonderland

1 Alice is a girl _____who_____ lives in England.
2 Alice falls into a world _____ strange people and things live.
3 Alice has adventures _____ she'll never forget.

Iron Man 2

4 Tony Stark is a billionaire _____ is also a superhero called Iron Man.
5 He has armor _____ is very hard and strong.
6 Everyone wants Tony to give them the armor _____ protects him.

THE LAST SONG

7 Ronnie is a girl _____ is unhappy because her parents divorced.
8 She moves to Georgia _____ her father lives.
9 She meets a handsome boy _____ helps her save sea turtles, and she falls in love.

Vocabulary: Types of movies

Now write the type of movie next to each movie title from the exercise above.

Alice in Wonderland = _____

Iron Man 2 = _____

The Last Song = _____

Unit 7

Lesson 7A, Grammar

Combine the sentences with *too* or *enough*.

1 This town is small. It doesn't have a theater.
   This town isn't big enough to have a theater.

2 New York is noisy. You can't sleep at night.
   _____

3 Mia doesn't live close. She can't visit often.
   _____

4 Jon isn't smart. He can't go to college.
   _____

5 Our car is big. We can't park it in that space.
   _____

6 He isn't rich. He can't buy anything he wants.
   _____

7 This food is hot. I can't eat it.
   _____

Lesson 7B

 Solve it!

It is Monday, March 13. Look at the information. Complete the conversation with the correct form of the verbs.

MOVIE: THE SCOOTER BOYS

Date: March 14 Time: 6:30 P.M.

2 ADULTS

Party!

Please come to my party
on March 17 at 6:00 P.M.
Address: 19 Cedar Road, Seattle
From Jane Kelly

Sounders vs Timbers
Saturday, March 18
2:30 P.M.   *Ben Watkins and David Watkins*

PGE Park, Portland, OR

Andy: What [1] ____*are you doing*____ (do) tomorrow?

Ben: I [2] _____ (go) to the
   _____ with my sister to
   see [3] _____.

Andy: Oh, OK. What [4] _____ (do)
   Friday?

Ben: Jane [5] _____ (have) a party
   at her house, and I'm going to that.
   [6] _____ you
   _____ (come), too?

Andy: No, [7] _____. I'm going to
   Paula's party. Are you free on Saturday?

Ben: No, I'm not. My father and
   I [8] _____ (drive) to Portland.

Andy: Why [9] _____ (go) there?

Ben: Because [10] _____ (play)
   against the Timbers. I'm really looking forward
   to it!

Lesson 7C, Use your English

Complete the conversation. Use the words and phrases in the box.

> • Anything else? • can I • for me, • I'd
> • 'll have • Me, too, • ~~What would you like?~~
> • Would you like

Waiter: [1] ____*What would you like?*____

Carlos: [2] _____ like
   steak, please.

Greg: And [3] _____ have
   ravioli, please?

Waiter: That's one steak and one ravioli.
   [4] _____

Carlos: Yes, I [5] _____ a green
   salad, too, please.

Waiter: [6] _____ something
   to drink?

Carlos: Orange juice [7] _____
   please.

Greg: [8] _____ please.

Unit 8

Lesson 8A, Vocabulary: Clothes, accessories, and styles

1 Look at the pictures, read the clues, and write the names of the boys.

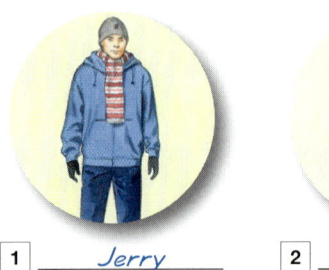

1 _Jerry_

2 _____

3 _____

4 _____

5 _____

- The weather's hot and sunny and Paul's clothes are right for the beach!
- Rob is going on a job interview.
- Mark's clothes are very casual, and he hates plain colors.
- Jerry is wearing clothes for cold weather.
- Tom is wearing only one color.

2 Now write sentences to describe what the boys are wearing.

1 _Jerry is wearing a blue sweatshirt ..._

2 _____

3 _____

4 _____

5 _____

Lesson 8B, Vocabulary: Personality adjectives

Read the clues and complete the crossword with personality adjectives.

Down

1 the opposite of loud
3 the opposite of cheap
5 the opposite of neat
8 the opposite of confident

Across

2 makes you laugh
4 never tells a lie
6 the opposite of rude
7 tells you what to do
9 will always be your friend
10 doesn't work hard

Lesson 8C, Grammar

Circle the correct words to complete the sentences.

1 A: What (is she like) / does she look like?

B: She's very funny.

2 He's *pretty / really* tall—almost seven feet!

3 Maria *wears / has* long, curly hair.

4 She's *a little / very* smart. She's a doctor.

5 A: *Are you like / Do you look like* your mother?

B: No. She's heavy, and I'm slim.

6 My father *is / has* well built.

Vocabulary: Physical appearance

Complete the paragraph with the correct word from the box.

> • beard • beautiful • eyeglasses • handsome
> • medium build • ordinary-looking • short
> • slim • ~~tall~~ • ugly • well

Meet the Smiths is a family sitcom about the Smiths. Tom and Sue Smith are a very ordinary couple. They are neither ¹ _tall_ nor ² _____ . Tom isn't thin or ³ _____ built, he is ⁴ _____ . Sue is neither ⁵ _____ nor heavy. Tom has a ⁶ _____ , and Sue wears ⁷ _____ . They aren't attractive, and they aren't ⁸ _____ , they are just ⁹ _____ . Their children, Adam and Karen, are different. Karen is a model. She's very ¹⁰ _____ , and Adam is very ¹¹ _____ , too. So what do ordinary Tom and Sue think about their extraordinary children? Watch the series and find out.

Unit 9

Lesson 9A, Grammar

Write true sentences in your notebook. Use *never* and the present perfect form of the verbs in the box.

> • be to • eat • ~~meet~~ • play/go • read • ride • see

1 a famous person
   I've never met the president.
2 a country   5 a food
3 a famous building 6 an animal
4 a sport   7 a book

Lesson 9B, Grammar

Ricardo is going camping with a friend. Look at Ricardo's list. In your notebook, make sentences with the cues in the list. Use *already* or *yet*.

1 Ricardo has already packed his suitcase.

Things to do before the festival
1 pack my suitcase ✓
2 buy some food ✓
3 clean my room ✗
4 find my tent ✓
5 make my bed ✗
6 make sandwiches ✗

Lesson 9C, Grammar

Write sentences. Use the words in parentheses.

1 He's gone out. (go out two minutes ago)
   He went out two minutes ago.
2 Carol is still doing her homework. (not finish yet)

   _____
3 I read that book two years ago. (already/read)

   _____
4 John doesn't know New York. (never/be)

   _____
5 I've already been to the U.S. (go last month)

   _____
6 I bought many guitars. (buy one/a few days ago)

   _____

Solve it!

Read the clues. Who likes rock music?

_____

1 Leo loves classical music.
2 Maria has never liked rock music.
3 Neither James nor Leo has ever bought any rap CDs.
4 Nora has just bought an R&B CD for Maria.
5 The person who likes rock is a boy.
6 Nora is a Jay-Z fan.

Unit 10

Lesson 10A, Grammar

Complete the conversations about the future with the correct form of *will*.

1 A: How ¹ _will_ we _get_ electricity? (we/get)
   B: We ² _____ power from the sun. (use)
2 A: ³ _____ cash for things? (people/pay)
   B: No, they ⁴ _____ . (not) They ⁵ _____ for everything with plastic cards. (pay)
3 A: What ⁶ _____ in the kitchen? (happen)
   B: Maybe ⁷ _____ to our stove (we/speak) and ⁸ _____ us a pizza! (it/make)
4 A: ⁹ _____ teachers? (there/be)
   B: Yes, there ¹⁰ _____ . (be) But they ¹¹ _____ to school every day. (not/come in)
5 A: How ¹² _____ to other countries? (a businessperson/travel)
   B: He or she ¹³ _____ . (not fly) The person ¹⁴ _____ by train or boat. (go)

Lesson 10B, Vocabulary: Computer language

Complete the words with the missing vowels.

1 sc_a_nn_e_r
2 m__m__ry st__ck
3 d__wnl__ __d
4 v__r__s
5 __tt__chm__nt

6 br__ __db__nd
7 d__skt__p c__mp__t__r
8 s__ftw__r__
9 k__yb__ __rd
10 l__pt__p

Grammar

In your notebook, write *if* clause + future sentences about Darren. The end of one sentence is the beginning of the next sentence.

1 If he loses his memory stick, he'll lose all his important files.
2 If he loses all his important files, . . .

1 he/lose his memory stick
2 he/lose all his important files
3 he/lose his school project
4 he/be in trouble with his teacher
5 his mom/not buy him a new pair of sneakers
6 he/not look cool
7 Nadia/not go to the school dance with him
8 Darren/not go to the dance

Lesson 10C, Vocabulary: Problems

Complete the sentence with the correct problem.

1 I'm sorry, but this CD is s_cratched_____ .
2 Look at this plate. It's c_____ .
3 This computer doesn't w_____ .
4 Oh, no! My jeans are t_____ !
5 What's w_____ with this radio?
6 The battery on my cell phone is d_____ .
7 I spilled coffee on my shirt and now it's s_____ .
8 Sorry, your favorite glass is b_____ .
9 We need to clean this table. It's d_____ .
10 One of the buttons on your shirt is m_____ .

Use your English

Number the sentences in the correct order. Then write the conversation in your notebook.

☐ Do you want me to try and fix it for you?
☐ The zipper's broken.
☐1 Mom, I have a problem with these jeans.
☐ Oh, thanks, Mom. That would be great.
☐ Yes, please. Here they are.
☐ I can't fix this. I'll put a new zipper in for you.
☐ What's the matter with them?

Unit 11
Lesson 11A, Grammar

Write conversations for each person in your notebook. Use the cues.

 1 Tania
 2 Armando
 3 Cole
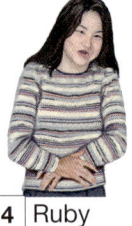 4 Ruby
 5 Bob
 6 Nina

1 eat any more sweet things ✗ /go to the dentist ✓

You: *What's the matter?*
Tania: *I have a toothache.*
You: *You shouldn't eat any more sweet things. You should go to the dentist.*

2 be at school ✗ /stay at home ✓
3 go to the doctor ✓ /wait for it to get better ✗
4 lie down ✓ /eat anything ✗
5 read any books ✗ /take a painkiller ✓
6 take some medicine ✓ /eat any chips ✗

Lesson 11B, Grammar

Complete the article about David Beckham with the correct form of *(not) have to* and the verbs.

| • be • go together • never/wear |
| • not/wash • put • take |

For David Beckham, a famous soccer player, everything [1]____*has to be*____ clean and perfect. When he goes into a hotel room, he changes everything. He [2]_____ everything in a straight line or in pairs. When he puts his soda cans in the fridge, if there's an odd number (e.g. 1, 3, or 5), he [3]_____ one away. He buys 20 pairs of socks every week, so his wife Victoria [4]_____ his socks, and he [5]_____ the same pair twice. What about his shirts and sweaters? [6]_____ they all [7]_____ the same color? No, they don't, but all the same colors [8]_____ in his closet!

Lesson 11C, Grammar

Complete the conversation with the correct past form of *have to* and the verbs in parentheses.

A: Did you hear? Tobey Maguire [1]*had to quit* (quit) the *Spider-Man* movies. So they're looking for a new actor to play Spider-Man.

B: Really? Well, they should choose someone strong. Tobey Maguire [2] _____ (train) for six months before he filmed the first movie.

A: Wow! [3] _____ (climb) a lot of tall buildings?

B: No, he [4] _____ (not/climb) them, silly! They used special computer effects for that!

A: Oh. What about the Spider-Man costume? [5] _____ (he/wear) that, or did they use special effects for that, too?

B: Well, he [6] _____ (wear) it most of the day. But he [7] _____ (not/wear) it when he was playing Peter Parker, of course. Then he wore normal clothes.

Unit 12

Lesson 12A, Vocabulary: Containers and materials

Complete the crossword with the correct material or container.

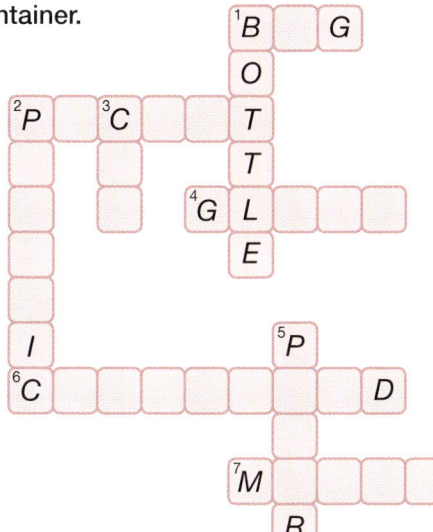

Lesson 12B, Vocabulary: Wild animals and insects

Label the pictures of the animals.

1 ___*hippo*___ 2 _____ 3 _____

4 _____ 5 _____ 6 _____

Grammar

Complete the sentences with *so . . . that* and the adjectives.

1 The weather was _____*so awful that*_____ (awful) we didn't go out.

2 The meal was _____ (big) I didn't finish it.

3 That movie was _____ (good) I saw it twice.

4 The test was _____ (easy) everyone passed it.

5 His backpack was _____ (cool) I bought one just like it.

Lesson 12C, Grammar

Answer the questions using *I'd prefer* or *I'd rather* and the cues.

1 Would you like to watch TV? (go to the movies)
   I'd prefer to go to the movies.

2 Should we leave now? (wait a few minutes)
   _____

3 Would you like to go out? (stay home)
   _____

4 Do you want to play a game? (read my book)
   _____

5 Do you want to play soccer? (swim)
   _____

6 Why don't you call him? (text him)
   _____

Word bank

Unit 1   1A Family
• grandfather • grandmother • father (dad) • mother (mom)
• brother • sister • son • daughter • husband • wife
• uncle • aunt • nephew • niece • stepfather
• stepmother • cousin(s) • parent(s) • grandparent(s)

1A Countries and nationalities
• Argentina/Argentinian • Australia/Australian
• Brazil/Brazilian • Canada/Canadian • Chile/Chilean
• China/Chinese • Colombia/Colombian • France/French
• Germany/German • Japan/Japanese • Mexico/Mexican
• Peru/Peruvian • Russia/Russian • Spain/Spanish
• the U.K./British • the U.S./American

1B Daily routines
• brush your teeth • call a friend • do your homework
• get home from school • get up • go to bed
• go to school • go to sleep • have breakfast
• have dinner • have lunch • leave school
• listen to music • play video games • read in bed
• take a shower • wake up • watch TV

The time
• 3:00 A.M.	three o'clock (in the morning)	3:00 P.M.	three o'clock (in the afternoon)
• 3:15	a quarter past (OR after) three	or	three fifteen
• 3:20	twenty (minutes) past (OR after) three	or	three twenty
• 3:30	half past three	or	three thirty
• 3:45	a quarter to four	or	three forty-five
• 3:50	ten (minutes) to four	or	three fifty

Note
12:00 in the day	twelve o'clock	or	midday
12:00 at night	twelve o'clock	or	midnight

1C Leisure activities
• chat with your friends online • go to a club/go clubbing
• go to a concert • go to the beach • go to the movies
• hang out with friends • have a barbecue • have a party
• jog/go jogging • listen to music • play video games
• play the guitar • surf the net • shop/go shopping
• swim/go swimming • watch a DVD

Unit 2   2A Jobs
• actor • administrative assistant • artist • builder
• chef • doctor • electrician • farmer • housewife
• model • musician • nurse • plumber • police officer
• reporter • store assistant • teacher • waiter/waitress

2B Money
• 60¢ = sixty cents/sixty ¢ • $1 = a/one dollar
• $5 = five dollars • $2.50 = two (dollars and) fifty (cents)
• $9.99 = nine (dollars and) ninety-nine (cents)

Everyday objects
• apple • bag • bike • book • camera • CD • cell phone
• diary • exercise book • hat • ID card • key • laptop
• pen • purse • sandwich • sneakers • T-shirt • watch

2C Food and drink
Fast food
• apple juice • burger • chicken sandwich • coffee
• cola • french fries • hot chocolate • hot dog
• ice cream • milk • mineral water • orange juice • tea

Other food and drink
• apple • banana • bread • butter • carrot • cheese
• chips • cookie • egg • fish • grape • honey • onion
• orange • pasta • pepper • potato • rice • salt
• sugar • tomato

Unit 3   3A Sports
Play • basketball • football • rugby • soccer • tennis
• volleyball **Go** • cycling • go-carting • motor racing
• skateboarding • skiing • snowboarding • swimming
• windsurfing **Do** • athletics • judo • karate
• gymnastics

Unit 4   4A Home and furniture
Rooms • attic • bathroom • bedroom • dining room
• hall • kitchen • living room • toilet
Parts of a house • door • downstairs • floor
• garage • upstairs • wall • window • yard
Appliances and features • bathtub • dishwasher
• refrigerator • shower • sink • stove • washing machine
Furniture • armchair • bed • bookcase • bureau
• carpet • CD player • chair • clock • computer
• cupboard • curtains • desk • DVD player • lamp
• mirror • plant • shelf • sofa • table • television (TV)
• wardrobe • wastepaper basket

Unit 5   5A Dates
Months • January • February • March • April
• May • June • July • August • September • October
• November • December

Ordinal numbers • 1st first • 2nd second • 3rd third
• 4th fourth • 5th fifth • 6th sixth • 7th seventh
• 8th eighth • 9th ninth • 10th tenth • 11th eleventh
• 12th twelfth • 13th thirteenth • 14th fourteenth
• 15th fifteenth • 16th sixteenth • 17th seventeenth
• 18th eighteenth • 19th nineteenth • 20th twentieth

Years
the nineteenth century   1831 eighteen thirty-one
the twentieth century   1900 nineteen hundred
1905 nineteen oh five   1989 nineteen eighty-nine
the twenty-first century   2000 two thousand
2001 two thousand and one   2010 twenty ten
2025 twenty twenty-five

Unit 6   6A The weather
• cold • cloud • cloudy • foggy • freezing • hot
• It's raining. • The sun's shining. • It's snowing. • sun
• sunny • warm • windy

6B Prepositions of location
• above • behind • between • in • in front of • on
• near • next to • on the corner of • opposite • under

Unit 7

7A Places in town

- bank • bookstore • café/coffee shop
- computer store • convenience store • drugstore
- factory • hospital • office • park • parking lot
- post office • restaurant • school • sports center
- station • supermarket • swimming pool

7B Transportation

- bike • boat • bus • car • motorcycle • plane
- scooter • subway • taxi • train • tram • truck

Unit 8

8A Clothes

- baseball cap • boots • coat • dress • hat • hoodie
- jacket • jeans • pants • sandals • shirt • shoes
- shorts • skirt • sneakers • socks • sweater
- sweatshirt • T-shirt • tights

8C Appearance

- beard • beautiful • blonde • curly • dark
- dark brown • fair • glasses • good-looking
- light brown • long • medium-height
- medium-length • middle-aged • mustache
- old • short • straight • tall • wavy • young

Unit 9

9A Vacation activities

- go climbing/climb • go mountain biking
- go shopping/shop • go sightseeing/sightsee
- go skiing/ski • go swimming/swim
- go to a museum • go to the beach
- go windsurfing/windsurf • play beach volleyball
- sunbathe

9C Types of music

- classical • country (and western) • folk • heavy metal
- hip-hop • jazz • latin • pop • R&B • rap • reggae
- rock • soul • techno

Unit 10

10B Computer language

Nouns: • broadband • file • Internet (net) • virus
- website

Verbs: • attach • burn • connect (to) • crash • delete
- download • open • print • receive • save
- search (for) • send • surf

Pronunciation

Unit 1

Lesson 1A Exercise 10

/ɪ/ l<u>i</u>ve, /i/ l<u>ea</u>ve

a 🎧 1 05 Listen and repeat.

live Brazil English it is isn't
leave speak three he she we

b 🎧 1 06 Listen and underline the /ɪ/ sounds and put a circle around the /i/ sounds.

1 He's from Brazil, but he speaks English.
2 Hi, Steve. Nice to meet you.
3 A: Is this your tea, Liz? B: No, it isn't.
4 I have three nieces, but they live in Argentina.

Unit 2

Lesson 2B Exercise 4

/ð/ <u>th</u>is, /θ/ <u>th</u>ink

a 🎧 1 15 Listen and repeat.

this that them they there
think three thirty thanks

b 🎧 1 16 Listen and underline the /ð/ sounds and put a circle around the /θ/ sounds.

1 There are thirty-three students in this class.
2 My brother is very good at math.
3 Thanks for that. I think it's great.
4 Excuse me. Where's the bathroom?

Unit 3

Lesson 3B Exercise 5

/ɛ/ l<u>e</u>g, /æ/ b<u>a</u>ck

a 🎧 1 30 Listen and repeat.

leg neck head chest
back ankle hand

b 🎧 1 31 Listen and underline the /ɛ/ sounds and put a circle around the /æ/ sounds.

1 Adam is a red belt, and Eddie is a black belt.
2 Can I have an egg and some bread for breakfast?
3 There's a math test next Wednesday.

Unit 4

Lesson 4A Exercise 6

/v/ <u>v</u>ase, /w/ <u>w</u>all

a 🎧 1 38 Listen and repeat.

vase very never living room volleyball
wall wastepaper basket window washing machine

b 🎧 1 39 Say the sentences. Then listen and check your pronunciation.

1 The vase in Wendy's living room is very big.
2 The wastepaper basket is over there, near the window.
3 It's never very windy in November.
4 When does Wayne want to play volleyball?

Unit 5

Lesson 5B Exercise 6

-ed endings

a 🎧 2 06 Listen and repeat these verbs.

answered /d/   discovered _____   hated _____
asked /t/   dropped _____   jumped _____
decided /ɪd/   happened _____   started _____

b 🎧 2 06 Listen again. How is the -ed ending of each verb pronounced? Write /ɪd/, /d/, or /t/ next to each verb in Exercise a above.

Unit 6

Lesson 6A Exercise 8

/ɑ/ h<u>o</u>t, /ɔr/ b<u>or</u>ed

a 🎧 2 12 Listen and repeat.

not hot want
bored warm four more

b 🎧 2 13 Listen and underline the /ɑ/ sounds and put a circle around the /ɔr/ sounds.

1 The water was warm, but it wasn't hot.
2 It was raining all morning.
3 Tom and Sonia did not arrive at four P.M.
4 What did Paul want?
5 He was bored.

Unit 7

Lesson 7C Exercise 3

/tʃ/ cheese, /ʃ/ fish

a [2 26] Listen and repeat.

cheese chicken chocolate french fries sandwich
sugar fish fresh fruit mashed potatoes

b [2 27] Listen and underline the /tʃ/ sounds and put a circle around the /ʃ/ sounds.

1 Chicken and mashed potatoes, please.
2 A fish sandwich, please.
3 Is the fish fresh?
4 French fries or mashed potatoes?
5 Chocolate ice cream or fresh fruit?

Unit 8

Lesson 8A Exercise 6

/tʃ/ checked, /dʒ/ jacket

a [2 34] Listen and repeat.

checked cheese child lunch watch
jacket jeans Japanese juice jump

b [2 35] Listen and underline the /tʃ/ sounds and put a circle around the /dʒ/ sounds.

1 Can I have a chicken sandwich and an apple juice, please?
2 John was wearing a checked shirt and jeans.
3 I had lunch in Los Angeles.
4 Jump out of the car! Now jog three times around the park!

Unit 9

Lesson 9B Exercise 5

/ʊ/ put, /u/ do

a [3 05] Listen and repeat.

put look cook wood
do who food too

b [3 06] Listen and underline the /ʊ/ sounds and put a circle around the /u/ sounds.

1 Look. I put some wood on the fire.
2 Let's cook some food.
3 Good! Who's going to cook?
4 Would you two do it?

Unit 10

Unit 10A Exercise 7

/aʊ/ now, /oʊ/ know

a [3 12] Listen and repeat.

now out how about brown
know go phone don't won't

b [3 13] Listen and underline the /aʊ/ sounds and put a circle around the /oʊ/ sounds.

1 How about a pizza in town before we go home?
2 Where is Howard now? I don't know.
3 Roland has a new phone.
4 Is the mountain road open?
5 He won't be at home now. He'll be out of town.

Unit 11

Lesson 11C Exercise 6

Word stress in two-syllable words

a [3 29] Listen and repeat.

sister dinner winner
forgot complain hotel
passport housework sandwich

b [3 30] Listen and underline the stressed syllable or syllables in these words.

homework believe airport away himself airline
mother table police rescue

Unit 12

Lesson 12C Exercise 5

Sentence stress

a [3 40] Listen and repeat.

I'd rather stand and watch.
He'd like to stay for lunch.
I hope to come in June.

b [3 41] Now listen and underline the stressed syllables in these sentences.

1 I'm here to say good-bye.
2 She'd like to leave tonight.
3 I'd rather call than write.
4 He wants to go by car.

Family life

Complete the example sentences and the grammar rules that follow.

Lesson 1A, page 4

Simple present

Affirmative	Negative
I **live** in New York. He **lives** in New York. We _____ in New York.	I **don't live** in Miami. He **doesn't live** here. We **don't live** in Miami.

Questions	Short answers
Do you **live** here?	Yes, I **do**./No, I _____.
Does she **live** here?	Yes, she **does**./No, she _____.
Where do they **live**?	In Seattle.

- For affirmative statements with *I, you, we,* and *they,* use the base form of the verb.
- For *he, she,* and *it,* use the base form of the verb + _____.
- For negative statements, use the short forms *don't* or _____ + the base form of the main verb.
- For *yes/no* questions, use this word order: *Do* or *Does* + the subject + the base form of the main verb.
- For information questions, use this word order: a *Wh-*word + *do* or *does* + the subject + the _____ of the main verb.

Lesson 1B, page 7

Adverbs and expressions of frequency

Adverbs

always usually often sometimes hardly ever never
100% ←——————————————————→ **0%**

Do you **sometimes** get up early?
I **never get up** early.
I **am never** late.

Expressions

How often do you play soccer?

I _____ it	**every /** **once a**	day/morning/ afternoon/evening.

- Adverbs of frequency usually go in the middle of the sentence, between the subject and the _____.
- Adverbs go _____ the verb *be*:
  *We **are never** late.*
- In questions, the adverb of frequency goes _____ the main verb.
- We put expressions of frequency such as *every day* at the _____ of the sentence.

Lesson 1C, page 9

Present continuous

Affirmative	Negative
I'm **playing** tennis right now. He**'s playing** a game now. We _____ **playing** football now.	I'm **not** _____ soccer right now. He **isn't** _____ tennis now. We **aren't playing** basketball now.

Questions	Short answers
_____ you _____ basketball?	Yes, I **am**./No, I'm **not**.
Is she **playing** a game?	Yes, she _____./ No, she _____.
What _____ he **doing**?	He**'s playing** a game.

- For affirmative statements, use am/are/is + the base form of the main verb + _____.
- For negative statements, use am/are/is + _____ + the base form of the main verb + -ing.
- The short form of *are + not* is _____. The short form of *is + not* is _____.
- For *yes/no* questions, use this word order: *Am/Is/Are* + a subject + the base form of the main verb + _____.
- For short answers, do not repeat _____:
  Yes, I am.
- For _____ questions, use a *wh-* word + *am/is/are* + a subject + the base form of the main verb + -ing.

Complete the example sentences and the grammar rules that follow.

Lesson 2A, page 13

Simple present	Present continuous
I **usually drink** coffee. You **wear** a T-shirt almost every day. He often _____ in an office.	I**'m drinking** tea today. You**'re** _____ a jacket today. He**'s working** at home right now.

- Use the _____ for daily habits or general statements of fact.
- Use the _____ to talk about things that are happening right now.
- Use the simple present with _____ such as *always*. Do not use the present continuous.

Lesson 2B, page 15

whose . . . ?	
Singular	**Plural**
Whose towel **is** that?	**Whose** CDs **are** those?

Possessive *'s* and *s'*	
Singular	**Plural**
It's my brother**'s** (towel). They're Mark_____ (CDs).	It's my parents**'** (towel). They're my brother____ (CDs).

Possessive adjectives	Possessive pronouns
It's **my** bag. It's _____ bag. It's **his** bag. It's _____ bag. It's **our** bag. It's _____ bag.	It's **mine**. It's **yours**. It's _____. It's **hers**. It's _____. It's **theirs**.

- Use _____ to ask questions about who owns or possesses something.
- Use a singular noun + *'s* or a plural noun + _____ to show ownership.
- Both possessive adjectives and possessive _____ show possession. They have the same meaning.
- A possessive _____ is followed by a noun. A possessive pronoun is used alone, without a noun.

Lesson 2C, page 17

Count and noncount nouns with *some*, *any*, and *no*	
Count (plural)	**Noncount**
Affirmative	
There **are some** tomatoes.	There**'s some** cheese.
Negative	
There **aren't any** pears. There **are no** pears.	There **isn't** _____ butter. There_____ **no** butter.
Questions	
Are there **any** cookies? **Is** there **any** chicken?	Yes, there _____./ No, there **aren't**. Yes, there **is**./No, there _____.

- A _____ noun can be singular or plural.
- A noncount noun has only one form. It has no _____ form.
- You can use *some*, *any*, and *no* with plural count nouns and with noncount nouns. You can't use *some*, *any*, or *no* with _____ count nouns.

Complete the example sentences and the grammar rules that follow.

Lesson 3A, page 23

Verbs of emotion + gerund (-*ing* form)

I **like listening** to music.
You **love** _____ video games.
He **hates** _____ soccer, but he **enjoys playing** tennis.
She **likes** ice skating, but she **doesn't** _____ skiing.
We **don't mind losing**.
They _____ **like standing** in the rain.
_____ you **prefer running** or **swimming**?

- Some verbs of emotion are followed by a _____.

- To form a gerund, use the base form of a verb + _____.

- For negative statements, use *don't* or _____ + a verb of emotion + a gerund.

Lesson 3B, page 25

Imperatives

Affirmative	Negative
Sit up.	**Don't sit** down.
Hold his arm.	_____ **hold** his neck.

- For affirmative imperatives, use the base form of the verb.
- For negative imperatives, use _____ + the base form of the verb.

must/must not for rules

Affirmative	Negative
You **must arrive** at 8 A.M.	You **must not be** late.
She **must stay** home tonight.	She **must not go** outside.

- For _____ sentences, use *must* + the base form of a verb.

- For negative sentences, use *must* + _____ + the base form of a verb.

Lesson 3C, page 27

be going to for future plans, intentions, and predictions

Affirmative

I**'m going to watch** a DVD.
He**'s** _____ **drink** coffee.
We**'re** _____ **pass** the test.
They**'re** _____ **swim**.

Negative

I**'m not going to watch** TV.
He _____ **drink** tea.
We _____ **fail** the test.
They **aren't going to ski**.

Questions	Short answers
What **is** he **going to do**?	**Go** swimming.
Are you **going to call** her?	Yes, I **am**./No, _____.

Future time phrases

- this morning / afternoon / evening
- tonight
- tomorrow
- on Saturday morning / afternoon / evening
- next week / month / year

- For affirmative statements, use a form of _____ + *going to* + the base form of a verb.
- For _____ statements, use a form of *be* + *going to* + *not* + the base form of a verb.
- For short answers to *yes/no* questions, use the subject + a form of _____. Do not repeat *going to* + the verb.
- Complete the example:
  Are you going to e-mail him? — Yes, _____.
- *This afternoon* and *next week* are examples of _____.

4 Places

Complete the example sentences and the grammar rules that follow.

Lesson 4A, page 31

Comparative and superlative forms of adjectives

Short adjectives

Base form	Comparative	Superlative
old	old**er**	old**est**
big	big**ger**	_____
happy	_____	hap**piest**

Long adjectives

Base form	Comparative	Superlative
modern	**more** modern	**most** _____

Irregular adjectives

Base form	Comparative	Superlative
good	**better**	**best**
bad	_____	**worst**
far	**farther**	**farthest**

It's **larger than** my house.
This is **the most expensive** hotel in the city.

- For most short adjectives, to form a comparative, add -er to the base form of the adjective. To form a superlative, add _____ to the base form of the adjective.
- When a short adjective ends in one vowel and a consonant, double the consonant and add -er or -est:
  big ➜ big**ger**.
- When a short adjective ends in y, change the y to _____ and add -er or -est:
  silly ➜ sill**ier**.
- For long adjectives, to form a _____, use more. To form a superlative, use _____.
- A comparative is followed by than. A _____ begins with the.

Lesson 4B, page 33

Count and noncount nouns with *much, many, a lot of, a few, a little*

Count	Noncount
There **are a lot of** students.	There **is a lot of** money in my bag.
There _____ **a few** students.	There **is a little** _____ in my bag.
There _____ many students.	There **isn't much** money in my bag.
Are there many students?	**Is there** _____ money in your bag?
How _____ **students** are there?	_____ **much money** is there in your bag?

- You can use _____ with both count and noncount nouns.
- Use a few with _____ nouns. Use a little with _____ nouns.
- Use many with count nouns. Use _____ with noncount nouns.
- Use How _____ to ask questions about count nouns. Use How _____ to ask questions about noncount nouns.

Lesson 4C, page 35

Question word *how* + adjectives of dimension

How high is it?	It's 10 feet **high**.
How _____ is it?	It's 50 feet **long**.
How wide is it?	_____ 200 feet **wide**.
How deep is it?	It's 100 feet _____.
How heavy is it? /	**It's**/It **weighs**
How much does it weigh?	100 pounds.
How far _____?	It's 10 miles.
_____ **big** is it?	It's **very big/not very big**.

- Use _____ + an adjective of dimension to ask questions about distances, heights, weights, etc.
- To answer a how question about dimension, you can drop or include the _____ in the answer.

Complete the example sentences and the grammar rules that follow.

Lesson 5A, page 41

Simple past of the verb *be*

Affirmative	Negative
I **was** in Miami.	I **wasn't** in Atlanta.
He **was** in San Francisco.	He _____ in Los Angeles.
We _____ in São Paulo.	We **weren't** in Rio de Janeiro.

Questions	Short answers
Were you in Chicago?	Yes, I **was**./ No, I **wasn't**.
Was she in Seattle?	Yes, she _____./ No, she **wasn't**.
_____ they in Orlando?	Yes, they **were**./No, they _____.

Past adverbial phrases

yesterday morning / afternoon
last night / week / month / year

- The past forms of *be* are *was* and _____.
- For statements about the past, use *was / were* + *not*. The short forms of *was not* and *were not* are _____ and _____.
- Use _____ phrases to talk about when something happened in the past:
  *We were in the city **last night**.*

Lesson 5B, page 42

Simple past of regular verbs

Affirmative	Negative
I **called** Ann.	I **didn't call** Maria.
He **carried** the backpacks.	He _____ **carry** the suitcases.

Questions	Short answers
Did you **play** a game?	Yes, I _____./ No, I **didn't**.
_____ they **play** soccer?	Yes, they **did**./ No, they _____.
What **did** you **play**?	A game.

- To form the simple past of most regular verbs, add _____ to the base form of the verb.
- If a verb ends in *y*, change the *y* to _____ and then add -*ed*.
- For negative statements in the past, use _____ + *not* + the base form of a verb. The short form of *did* + *not* is _____.
- For *yes/no* questions, use this word order: *Did* + subject + the base form of a verb.
- For information questions, use this word order: a *Wh-word* + _____ + subject + the base form of a verb.

Lesson 5C, page 45

Simple past of irregular verbs

Affirmative	Negative
I **ate** a sandwich.	I **didn't eat** pizza.
You **made** a cake.	You **didn't make** bread.
He **told** the truth.	He _____ **tell** a lie.
She **gave** me a card.	She **didn't give** me a present.
We **did** our homework.	We _____ **do** the dishes.
They **went** to Argentina.	They _____ to Chile.

Questions	Short answers
Did you **take** the bus?	Yes, I _____./ No, I **didn't**.
When **did** you **write** the e-mail?	(I **wrote** it) at 11 o'clock.

Adverbial phrases with *ago*

She got up **an hour ago**.	We bought a TV **three weeks** _____.

- Some verbs have irregular past forms. Go to www.pearsonlongman.com/insync/grammarreference for a list of irregular verbs and their past forms.
- Use *ago* to talk about when something happened. *Ago* goes _____ the adverbial phrase: *an hour ago.*

6 Stories

Complete the example sentences and the grammar rules that follow.

Lesson 6A, page 49

Past continuous

Affirmative	Negative
I **was playing** tennis at 10 A.M.	I **wasn't playing** soccer.
You **were wearing** a sweater yesterday.	You **weren't** _____ a sweatshirt.
He _____ **listening** to music at 3 P.M.	He **wasn't listening** to his friend.
She **was calling** her mother at 4 P.M.	She _____ **calling** her father.
We _____ at the mall last night.	We **weren't shopping** at the supermarket.
They **were waiting** for the bus at 8 A.M.	They _____ for the train.

Questions	Short answers
Were you **cleaning** your room at 11 A.M.?	Yes, I _____./ No, I **wasn't**.
_____ they _____ basketball?	Yes, they **were**./ No, they **weren't**.
Where were they **playing** basketball?	At the park.

- Use the _____ to talk about an action that was in progress or was happening at a particular point of time in the past.
- For affirmative statements, use *was* or _____ + the *-ing* form of the main verb.
- For negative statements, use *was* or *were* + _____ + the *-ing* form of the main verb.
- For *yes/no* questions, use _____ + the subject + the *-ing* form of the main verb.
- For information questions, use a *wh*-word + *was* or *were* + the subject + the *-ing* form of the main verb.

Lesson 6B, page 50

Past continuous and simple past with *while* and *when*

While we **were watching** TV, Paul called.
We were watching TV **when** Paul **called**.
While I **was doing** my homework, I fell asleep.
When I _____ asleep, I _____ my homework.

- Use the past continuous with the simple past to talk about an action that happened at the same time as another action. Use the past continuous for the longer action that was "in progress." Use _____ for the shorter, finished action.
- *While* means "during that time." *When* means "at that time." We usually use *while* with the _____ tense. We usually use *when* with the _____ tense.
- Complete this example:
  _____ *Ann was eating lunch, the phone rang.*

Lesson 6C, page 53

Adjective clauses with *who, that,* and *where*

People (*who* or *that*)
The movie is about a man **who**/**that** travels to the moon.

Things (_____)
The movie is about a plane **that** crashes.

Places (*where*)
The woman goes to an apartment _____ she talks to a family.

- Use an adjective clause to describe or give information about a noun.
- *Who, that,* and *where* are relative pronouns. Use _____ or *that* to talk about people. Use *that* to talk about _____. Use *where* to talk about _____.

Complete the example sentences and the grammar rules that follow.

Lesson 7A, page 59

too + adjective	*not* + adjective + *enough*
The town is **too small**.	The town is**n't big enough**.

too + adjective + infinitive	*not* + adjective + *enough* + infinitive
It's **too expensive to buy** a ticket.	It's **not cheap enough to buy** a ticket.

- *Too* with an adjective means "more than necessary." It has a negative meaning.
- *Enough* means "sufficient" or "the right amount." It has a positive meaning. *Not* _____ means "too little" and has a negative meaning.
- Use *too* before an adjective. Use *enough* _____ an adjective.
- Both *too* + adjective and *not* + adjective + *enough* can be followed by an _____:
  It's too expensive **to buy** *a ticket*.

Lesson 7B, page 61

Present continuous for future plans

Questions	Answers
What **are** you **doing** this weekend?	**I'm visiting** my aunt.
_____ you **going** by car?	_____, **I am**./ No, **I'm not**.
Who **is going** with you?	My mother.
_____ your father **coming**, too?	No, he **isn't**. He _____ **staying** at home.

- Use the _____ to talk about plans that people have made for the future.
- Use time markers like *this weekend, tomorrow,* etc. with present continuous verbs to talk about future plans:
  I'm going to the movies **tomorrow**.

Lesson 7C, page 62

like and *would like*

like	
I **like** spaghetti. He **likes** shrimp.	I **don't like** rice. He **doesn't** _____ steak.
Do you **like** apple pie? **Does** she _____ ice cream?	Yes, I **do**./No, I **don't**. Yes, she _____./ No, she **doesn't**.

would like	
I**'d like** mashed potatoes, please. **Would** you **like** a salad?	She**'d like** french fries. Yes, please./ No, thanks.

- Use *like/likes* to talk about things you always like. Use *would like* to talk about things you want right now.
- Use _____ like to make offers or order food in a restaurant. It is a polite way to ask for things or to say what you want.
- _____ is the short form of *I would*. The short form of *he would* is _____.
- For *he/she* sentences with *would like*, do not change the base form of the verb.
- Complete this example:
  He'd _____ *an apple*.

8 Friends

Complete the example sentences and the grammar rules that follow.

Lesson 8A, page 67

Indefinite pronoun *one/ones*

Singular

Which **one** do you like?	The **one** with red stripes. This **one**. That _____. The big blue **one**.

Plural

Which **ones** do you like?	The ones with zippers. The blue _____.

- Use *one* or *ones* to replace a singular or plural count noun when people know what you are talking about:
  *Which **shirt** do you like? = Which **one** do you like?*
- *One* is singular. *Ones* is _____.
- Use *this/that* before _____. Use *these/those* before _____. You can use _____ before both *one* and *ones*.

Lesson 8B, page 69

Conditional: *if* clause + present

Questions	Answers
What **do** you **do** if it **is** your birthday?	**If** it**'s** my birthday, I **have** a party.
What **does** he **do** if it **rains**?	He _____ go out _____ it **rains**.
Do you **watch** TV if you **have** time?	Yes, I **do**./No, I **don't**.

- Use an *if* clause + _____ to talk about true situations and general facts or rules. Use the simple present tense in the *if* clause:
  If it is cloudy, it usually rains.
- In sentences with an *if* clause and a main clause, the *if* clause can go in the first part or second part of the sentence.
- Complete the example:
  What do you do if the train _____ late?

Lesson 8C, page 71

be like and *look like*

to be like (personality)

What **is** he **like**? What **are** you **like**? **Are** they _____ their brothers?	He**'s** very smart. I**'m** a little shy. Yes, they **are**./No, they _____.

to look like (appearance)

What **does** he **look like**? What **do** you _____? **Do** they **look** _____ their brothers?	He**'s** kind of thin./ He **has** black hair./ He **wears** eyeglasses. I**'m** pretty tall. Yes, they _____./ No, they **don't**.

- Use *be like* to talk about someone's personality. Use _____ to talk about someone's appearance.
- Use forms of *be* for questions and answers with *be like*:
  A: **Are** *you like your sister?*
  B: *Yes, I **am**.*
- Use forms of *do* for questions with _____:
  *What **does** your sister look like?*
- Use adverbs like _____, *pretty, a little, kind of*, and *really* before an adjective to talk about both personality and appearance. These adverbs make an adjective stronger or weaker.
- Complete this example:
  A: *What _____ she _____ _____?*
  B: *She's very pretty.*

Complete the example sentences and the grammar rules that follow.

Lesson 9A, page 77

Present perfect

Affirmative	Negative
I **have**/I've been to the U.S. You_____ **visited** Brazil. He's **tried** surfing. We've **seen** a mountain. They've _____ in a hotel.	I **have not**/**haven't been** to the U.K. You **haven't visited** Chile. He **hasn't** _____ whale-watching. We **haven't** _____ a volcano. They **haven't slept** in a tent.

Questions	Answers
Have you **been** to Colombia? **Has** she **met** Selena Gomez?	Yes, I **have.**/ No, I **haven't.** Yes, she **has.**/ No, she _____.

Present perfect with *ever* and *never*

Ever: Questions	*Never:* Negative
Have you **ever been** to Peru? **Has** she _____ **met** Selena Gomez? **Have** they **ever seen** Taylor Lautner?	No. I've **never been** to Peru. No. She_____ **never met** Selena Gomez. No. They've **never** _____ Taylor Lautner.

- For affirmative statements, use *have* or *has* + the past participle of the main verb.
- For negative statements, use *have* or *has* + *not* + the past participle.
- For *yes/no* questions, use *has* or _____ + the past participle.
- *Ever* means "at any time." Use *ever* with present perfect _____. Do not use *ever* with affirmative or negative statements.
- *Never* means "not ever." Use *never* for _____ present perfect statements. *Never* goes before the past participle.

Lesson 9B, page 78

Present perfect with *already* and *yet*

Affirmative	Negative
I've **already eaten** breakfast. You've **already** _____ a shower.	I **haven't eaten** breakfast **yet.** You **haven't taken** a shower _____.

Questions	Short answers
Has she **taken** a shower **yet**? **Have** they **arrived** _____?	Yes, she **has.**/No, she _____. Yes, they_____./ No, they **haven't.**

- For affirmative present perfect statements, use *has* or *have* + *already* + the past participle of the main verb.
- For negative statements, use *have* or *has* + *not* + the past participle of the main verbs + *yet*.
- *Already* can go between *have/has* and the past participle. *Yet* goes _____ the past participle.
- For *yes/no* questions, use *has* or _____ + subject + past participle + *yet*. *Yet* usually goes at the end of the question.

Lesson 9C, page 81

Simple past	Present perfect
I **went** to a concert last Saturday. She _____ Ecuador in 2009. We **made** a CD last year. They **listened** to the CD last night. **Did** you **write** a song yesterday? Yes, I **did.**/No, I **didn't.**	I've **gone** to many concerts. She's **never visited** Ecuador. We've _____ **made** a CD. They **haven't** _____ to the CD **yet.** **Have** you **ever written** a song? Yes, I **have.**/No, I ____.

- Use the simple past for actions that happened at a specific time in the past, such as *last Saturday*.
- Use the _____ to talk about actions that happened at an unspecified time in the past, for actions that happened more than once, and for past activities that aren't finished yet.
- Complete the example:
  _____ *she ever gone fishing?*

10 Technology

Complete the example sentences and the grammar rules that follow.

Lesson 10A, page 85

will for predictions

Affirmative	Negative
I'll (will) go on vacation this summer.	I won't (will not) be in school tomorrow.
You'll have one child.	You won't _____ many children.
She'll buy a bicycle.	She won't buy a car.
_____ live on the earth in the future.	We won't _____ on the moon.
Robots will clean our homes.	They _____ clean our bodies.

Questions	Answers
Will robots clean our homes?	Yes, they will. / No, they won't.
What won't robots _____?	Our bodies.

- Use *will* for predictions about things that will happen in the future.
- For affirmative statements, use *will* + _____ of the main verb.
- For _____ statements, use *will* + *not* + the base form of the main verb.
- The short form of *you will* is _____. The short form of *will not* is _____.
- For short answers to *yes/no* questions with *will* and *won't,* do not repeat the _____.
- Complete the example:
  A: *Will robots teach our children?*
  B: *No, they _____.*

Lesson 10B, page 87

Conditional: *if* clause + future

Affirmative	Negative
If I have time, I'll help you.	_____ you get sick, you won't go to school.
If she texts me, I'll answer her.	They won't be late if they leave now.

Questions	Answers
Will you go to school if you get sick?	Yes, I will. / No, I won't.
What will you do _____ you get sick?	I'_____ take some medicine.

- Use an *if* clause + the future tense to talk about actions that will happen in the future as long as something else happens. This structure describes real situations that are likely to happen.
- Use the _____ tense in the *if* clause and *will* or *won't* in the main clause.
- Complete the example:
  If I lose the race, I _____ get a prize.

Lesson 10C, page 88

will for decisions and promises

I'll (will) call him later.	I won't forget.
I _____ do my homework later.	I _____ watch TV.

will for offers

He'll buy you a soda.

- Use *will* for _____ made at the time of speaking:
  A: *Is Juan here?*
  B: *I don't know. I'll check.*
- Use *will* for _____ to take future action:
  I'll fix your computer this weekend.
- You can also use *will* for _____ to do something:
  I'll buy you a hot dog.

Complete the example sentences and the grammar rules that follow.

Lesson 11A, page 95

should / shouldn't	
Affirmative	**Negative**
I **should go** home now.	I **shouldn't (should not) stay** out late.
You **should take** some medicine.	You **shouldn't go** to work today.
He **should do** his homework.	He _____ **watch** TV.
We **should go** home.	We _____ **go** out.
They _____ **listen** to the teacher.	They _____ **fall asleep** in class.
Questions	**Answers**
Should I **go** to the doctor?	Yes, you **should.** / No, you **shouldn't.**
What **should** they **do**?	They _____ **study**.

- Use *should/shouldn't* to give advice or to talk about what is right or wrong to do.
- For affirmative statements, use _____ + the base form of the main verb. For negative statements, use *shouldn't* + _____.
- *Should* does not have a short form. The short form of *should not* is _____.

Lesson 11B, page 97

have to/don't have to	
Affirmative	**Negative**
I **have to go** home at 7 P.M.	I **don't have to go** home now.
You **have to get up** at 6 A.M.	You **don't have** _____ **get** up at 5 A.M.
She **has to do** the dishes every night.	She **doesn't** _____ **vacuum**.
We **have to do** the laundry.	We _____ **take out** the garbage.
Questions	**Answers**
Do I **have to stay** home tonight?	Yes, you **do.** / No, you **don't.**
What **does** he **have to do**?	He _____ **stay home**.

- Use *have to* to talk about necessity, or things that someone needs to do. *Have to* is stronger than *should*.
- Use *don't have to* to talk about things that aren't necessary to do.
- For affirmative statements, use *have to* or *has to* + the base form of the main verb.
- For negative statements, use _____ or *doesn't* + *have to* + the base form of the main verb.
- *Have to* does not have a short form. The short form of *do not have to* is _____.
- For questions, use *do/does* + subject + _____ + the base form of the main verb.

Lesson 11C, page 98

had to/didn't have to	
Affirmative	**Negative**
You **had to get** up at 6 A.M. yesterday.	You _____ **have** _____ **get** up on Sunday.
He **had to do** the dishes last night.	He **didn't** _____ **vacuum**.
Questions	**Answers**
Did you **have to stay** home last night?	Yes, I **did.** / No, I _____.
What **did** she **have to do** last year?	She _____ **study** English.

- Use *had to* to talk about past necessity. Use _____ to talk about things that weren't necessary to do in the past.
- For affirmative statements, use _____ + the base form of the main verb.
- For negative statements, use _____ + the base form of the main verb.
- *Had to* does not have a short form. The short form of *did not have to* is _____.

Complete the example sentences and the grammar rules that follow.

Lesson 12A, page 103

Infinitives of purpose

I'm going shopping **to buy** some food.
They searched the Internet **to find** information about recycling.
Did you go to the library _____ **check** out some books?

- Use infinitives of purpose to give a purpose or reason for doing something.
- For statements of purpose, use a main clause (subject + verb) + _____ + the base form of a verb.

Lesson 12B, page 105

so + adjective + that

It was **so** hot **that** I went swimming.
Some animals are **so** dangerous _____ people are scared of them.
The chimpanzee was _____ intelligent **that** it learned to communicate with people.

- Use *so* + adjective + *that* to talk about extremes that lead to certain results.
  *It was **so** hot **that** I went swimming. = It was very hot, and for that reason I went swimming.*
- *So* goes _____ the adjective. *That* goes _____ the adjective.

Lesson 12C, page 107

would ('d) rather	would ('d) prefer
I'd (would) rather **stay** home **than go** for a walk.	I'd **prefer to stay** home.
We'd **rather not go** for a walk.	We'd **prefer not to go** for a walk.
You'd **rather sleep than** exercise.	You'd **prefer to sleep**.
You'd **rather not exercise**.	You'd **prefer not to exercise**.
She'd **rather sunbathe** _____ **swim**.	She'd _____ **sunbathe**.
She'd _____ **not swim**.	She'd _____ to **swim**.

Questions	Answers
Would you **rather go skiing** or **skating**?	I'd **rather go skiing**. / **Skiing**.
Would you **prefer to go skiing**?	Yes, I **would**. / No, I **wouldn't**.
Would he **prefer** _____ **go skating**?	Yes, he _____. / No, he _____.
What **would** they **prefer to do**?	They'd **prefer to go skiing**.

- Use *would rather* and *would prefer* to talk about preferences, when you like one activity more than another. Use *rather* when choosing between options.
- For *would rather* statements, use *would ('d)* + *rather* + (*not*) + the base form of a verb.
- For *would prefer* statements, use *would ('d)* + *prefer* + (*not*) + _____ + base form of a verb.
- Use *than* after *rather* to state a preference between two options:
  *I'd rather swim **than** sunbathe.*
- Do not repeat *rather* or *prefer* in short answers.

CLIL PROJECTS

Go to www.pearsonlongman.com/insync/projects

CLIL PROJECT 1D, page 11
Social Studies

PAIRS Discuss: What are the favorite free-time activities of teenagers in your country? Then make a poster. Go to the website above, find CLIL Project 1D, and print out the instructions.

CLIL PROJECT 2D, page 19
Nutrition

GROUPS Discuss: What do teenagers in your country like to eat? Then do a survey about your classmates' eating habits. Go to the website above, find CLIL Project 2D, and print out the instructions.

CLIL PROJECT 3D, page 29
Physical Education

PAIRS Brainstorm sports from your country. Then write a description of a sport. Go to the website above, find CLIL Project 3D, and print out the instructions.

CLIL PROJECT 4D, page 37
Geography

GROUPS List famous historical landmarks. Then make a poster about a landmark. Go to the website above, find CLIL Project 4D, and print out the instructions.

CLIL PROJECT 5D, page 47
History

PAIRS Brainstorm a list of famous historical events. Then choose a historical event and research what happened. Go to the website above, find CLIL Project 5D, and print out the instructions.

CLIL PROJECT 6D, page 55
English / Literature

PAIRS Discuss: What is your favorite movie or book? What happened in it? Then write a sequel for it. Go to the website above, find CLIL Project 6D, and print out the instructions.

CLIL PROJECT 7D, page 65
Social Studies

PAIRS Discuss: What are your favorite foods and places to eat? Then make a collage about them. Go to the website above, find CLIL Project 7D, and print out the instructions.

CLIL PROJECT 8D, page 73
Ethics

PAIRS Brainstorm a list of English songs about friendship. Then choose one and explain its words or lyrics. Go to the website above, find CLIL Project 8D, and print out the instructions.

CLIL PROJECT 9D, page 83
Ethics

GROUPS Discuss: What is a *team*? Do you like working in a team? Why or why not? Then make a poster about teamwork. Go to the website above, find CLIL Project 9D, and print out the instructions.

CLIL PROJECT 10D, page 91
Science / Technology

PAIRS Discuss: How do you think people will communicate with each other in the future? Then invent a new way for people to communicate. Go to the website above, find CLIL Project 10D, and print out the instructions.

CLIL PROJECT 11D, page 101
Health

PAIRS Make a list of common illnesses. Then make a poster about how to treat them. Go to the website above, find CLIL Project 11D, and print out the instructions.

CLIL PROJECT 12D, page 109
Environmental Studies / Science

PAIRS Discuss: What environmental problems do people need to solve in your country? Then give a presentation about solving an environmental problem. Go to the website above, find CLIL Project 12D, and print out the instructions.